Excellence in Education

EXCELLENCE
IN THE STATES TAKE CHARGE
EDUCATION

Denis P. Doyle and Terry W. Hartle

American Enterprise Institute for Public Policy Research
Washington, D.C.

Library of Congress Cataloging in Publication Data

Doyle, Denis P.
  Excellence in education.

  (AEI studies ; 424)
  1. Education and state—United States.
2. State aid to education—United States. 3. Education
—United States—Aims and objectives. I. Hartle,
Terry W. II. Title III. Series.
LC89.D69   1985   379.73   85-15731
ISBN 0-8447-3580-9 (alk. paper)
AEI Studies 424

1 3 5 7 9 10 8 6 4 2

Printed in the United States of America

Contents

Presidentʼs foreword   vii

Foreword   xi

1   Introduction   1

2   The Context of Reform: The Capabilities and   4
Interests of State Governments
   Improving the Machinery of State Government   4
   The Statesʼ Interest in the Quality of Education   7
   The Quality of Education Can Be Improved   11
   Education for Economic Growth   13

3   Recent Efforts by States to Reform   19
Education
   Teachers   19
   The Academic Experience   24
   Increased Financial Support for Education   29
   Education Organization and Structure   33
   Federal Initiatives   37

4   The Next Phase: Implementing the   39
Reforms
   Short-Term Issues   39
   Long-Term Issues   48
   The Future of Education Reform: An Agenda   57

5   Conclusion   61

Notes   68

President's Foreword

This timely book is a product of AEI's 1984 Public Policy Week, an annual gathering of scholars, policy analysts, policy makers, and business leaders. Before an audience of two hundred and fifty participants, Governors Lamar Alexander (R.-Tenn.) and Charles Robb (D.-Va.), California superintendent of Public Instruction Bill Honig, and Florida state Senator Jack Gordon were asked by AEI's Education Policy Studies program to address the question of how the states were responding to the education excellence "movement."

No better qualified panel could have been assembled to discuss the issues of education excellence at the state and local level. Each member has played a leading role in his own state and is nationally recognized as a leader in education reform. And each holds distinctive and provocative ideas about the meaning of the excellence movement and how it should be treated. In preparation for that session, AEI's Denis P. Doyle and Terry W. Hartle prepared a paper that outlined what state governments had already accomplished and described the challenges that lay ahead. This volume is an expanded and revised version of that paper.

Excellence in Education: The States Take Charge represents a new emphasis for the American Enterprise Institute. Its focus on the states rather than the federal government reflects the changing domestic realities of the 1980s. The domestic policy role of Washington, which not long ago was accelerating, is giving way to the states. The change is occurring for two reasons. First, federal budget pressure is diminishing the capacity of the federal government to be all things to all people.

Second, and more important, the states today are at once more competent, more skillful, and more sophisticated than at any time in our history. They are doing more in education because they have the institutional competence to do so; they have the resources and they have the will. It is a potent combination.

This development is of the utmost importance in the 1980s because it is becoming clear that Washington cannot accomplish all that it set out to do in the sixties. Federal policy in too many areas has produced an Uncle Sam who is jack of all trades and master of none. Recognizing this, the Reagan administration and a number of state governors, Democrats as well as Republicans, attempted to fashion a "New Federalism," a sorting out of responsibilities between Washington and state capitols. The conventional wisdom, however, is that "New Federalism" was a failure—the states refused to co-operate.

But as Doyle and Hartle point out, if it did not get enacted formally, New Federalism—in education at least—is a reality today in all but name. Helter skelter, without benefit of centralized planning, Washington's role in education is decreasing and the role of the states is increasing in importance. As the authors observe:

> In a very real sense, then, the first four years of the Reagan administration have been a triumph of education policy, although hardly one that was planned. Through federal budget policy the states have been starved, not into submission, but into self reliance.

The shift from the federal government to state government does not mean that education is no longer a national issue. Education is today more than ever central to the nation's well being. But the shift to the states means that the problems and opportunities before us will be confronted differently than they would have been had Washington's role increased in importance. Indeed, the diversity and variety of America's "system" of public schools gives new meaning to the notion of "let a thousand flowers bloom." The nation's 40 million public school students are educated in more than 15,000 school districts; overseeing these schools are more than 80,000 school trustees; the schools employ 2.1 million teachers and spend more than $120 billion each year. In addition to the fifty governors and fifty chief state school officers there are 7,000 state legislators, many of whom have a strong interest in education. It should be no surprise that a system so vast and so diverse does not lend itself to centralized orchestration and management from Washington.

The issue today, of course, is more than management of the schools. As the nation's attention turns to the question of education excellence, it is clear that the federal government can play only a marginal role in school improvement. The issues of excellence are by their very nature best suited to state and local resolution. Questions of teacher competence, conditions of work and compensation, student performance and measurement, the quality of textbooks, local and regional curricular needs are all state and local issues. Washington has neither the ability nor the resources to deal effectively with these issues.

But if Washington is unable to meet the nation's demand for better schools, can the states do so? As the authors point out, there are two dimensions to the answer. One has to do with the institutional competence of state governments to deal with the analytic and political challenges posed by the excellence movement. Do they have the intellectual and physical resources to systematically examine and solve a set of complex and demanding problems? Doyle and Hartle argue that many states do. They indicate, as well, that acquiring these resources is within the reach of the other states.

Indeed, some states are so competent that an altogether different problem emerges. Will state legislators and governors have the self-restraint to avoid becoming overly intrusive? The lessons of contemporary education research are very clear—lasting school reform is a process that builds from the bottom up, school room by school room, school building by school building. Bureaucracy and centralized education decision making are hostile to good education.

Second, there remains the question of implementation. Now that the responsibility for education rests more squarely in state capitols and local school districts how will they meet their obligations to students? Will the nation as a whole be served by the emergence of states as senior partners in the education system? The jury, of course, is still out. And while the authors are optimistic about the capacity of states to lead, the answer to the question is an empirical one. Over the next several years the authors will try to answer to that question which, we hope, will be the subject of another book.

WILLIAM J. BAROODY, JR.
President
American Enterprise Institute

Foreword

In the following pages, Denis Doyle and Terry Hartle present a timely, straightforward, and laudably brief description and analysis of the amazing activity of the states in making education policy during the past two years. Since the many, much-publicized national reports and studies began appearing in 1983, governors, state legislatures, and state education agencies have launched a veritable revolution in elementary and secondary education policy. Working at a pace unprecedented in education since the federal government's launching of the Great Society in 1965, state officials have changed and raised the standards and requirements for curriculum and instruction and have developed new policies and programs to train, pay, promote, retrain, and evaluate teachers.

Without sounding flashy or facile, Doyle and Hartle have reduced what must be roomsful of documents generated by these policy charges to concise, clearly written paragraphs. They do not hide their approval of most of the state initiatives; but they note faithfully that critical concerns persist about the overuse or misuse of tests for students and teachers, about accepting too gratefully the renewed interest of corporations in education, and, most important, about possible adverse effects of the new education policy agenda on equity in education.

Along with their descriptive tour, Doyle and Hartle put forth several judgments about the deeper and more lasting significance of the whirlwind of state action. They note that:

• states have been developing the political, administrative, and financial capacity for their new role for two decades
• the wave of activity rests on the revived assumption, coming from both new research and a rediscovered common sense, that schools do make a difference in the individual and common life and can be improved
• the new state role does not eliminate the necessary role of the federal government. To the contrary, through the Voting Rights Act of 1965, other legislative and judicial action in pursuit of civil rights, and funding for programs promoting equal educational opportunity

and research, the federal government has compelled the states to become more competent, more active, and more attentive to the requirements of equal education for all. This state response is most certainly a prominent part of the "Reagan Revolution," but it rests upon an earlier revolution in federalism

• the expanded state role is creating an important reorganization of the states' relationships with local school districts and with individual schools, producing a threefold effect: more regulation of local districts, development of educational improvement strategies at the school building level, and incentives for professional autonomy and performance by teachers. This mixture could be unstable if not combustible if states, localities, and the leaders of teacher organizations do not deal sensitively with the changes involved in relationships among themselves and within the districts and school buildings

Doyle and Hartle demonstrate beyond question that state policymakers, with strong public support so far, are creating opportunities and resources for educators to improve the schools. They also suggest, probably more gently than they should, that the process will be more uncomfortable than most of us have yet realized. The mandated changes in programs may be difficult, internally inconsistent, and occasionally unwise, and the implied changes in the locus and style of educational leadership are largely unrecognized. From this perspective, the *next* few years will be more important than the past two in ensuring a successful era of education reform.

P. MICHAEL TIMPANE
President
Teachers College, Columbia University

1
Introduction

The last two years have witnessed the greatest and most concentrated surge of educational reform in the nation's history. According to the U.S. Department of Education,

> deep public concern about the Nation's future created a tidal wave of school reform which promises to renew American education. Citizens, perplexed about social, civic, and economic difficulties, turned to education as an anchor of hope for the future of their nation and their children. The schools survived an unprecedented firestorm of critical comment and attention from the press to emerge at the end of the year with greater public support than at any time in the recent past.[1]

During this period, state and local governments launched a dizzying number of efforts to improve the schools.

Indeed, the most surprising aspect of the "tidal wave" of reform is that it came from state governments. For the last twenty-five years, beginning with the launching of Sputnik and the proclamation of the Great Society, the federal government took the lead in education reform, offering legislation and money to encourage change at the state and local levels. This time the federal government provided some of the stimulus, and state governments produced new legislation, policy initiatives, and funding.

The modest role played by the national government should not come as a surprise. Although federal initiatives have been important strategic developments, particularly in the area of civil rights, Americans too often overemphasize Washington's role in education policy. Education has always been primarily the responsibility of the states, a product of historical development, public preference, and the reserve powers clause of the Constitution. At the state level, each constitution spells out, often in great detail, state responsibilities and obligations.

The federal role in education is permitted by the commerce clause, which allows federal expenditures of funds for public purposes. The commerce clause, however, does not mandate compliance. As a result most federal education programs are conditional. They operate on the "condition" that recipients comply with federal guidelines: no compliance, no money. The notable exceptions are the Education of All Handicapped Children Act (P.L. 94–142), and Title IX of the Higher Education Act, both of which mandate compliance as a civil right.

Although the states are not autonomous, neither are they creatures of the federal government. No such relationship characterizes the state and local school boards. To the contrary, local school boards are creatures of state governments, and they exist at the pleasure of the state. As long as the lion's share of school funding came from localities, this formal distinction had limited importance. As a general rule, states left local districts to their own devices in almost direct proportion to the amount of money they raised.

But the state role is growing. Three trends give special meaning to this observation. First, most state governments have, for a wide variety of reasons, increased the amount of money they spend relative to local expenditures. Second, court-ordered school finance reform has had a major impact in many places, leading many states to equalize educational expenditures between school districts. Third, state legislatures care more about education than they have at any previous time in their history, in part because they are spending more money on it, in part because they recognize its importance to economic growth and social progress. As state legislatures provide more money and exercise more oversight, local districts run the risk of losing both autonomy and flexibility.

This is not, of course, to deny the role played by the federal government and local school districts. The old adage remains true: Education is a national concern, a state responsibility, and a local function. Yet despite the federal role in helping shape the agenda and the local role in delivering the service, the role of state government grows increasingly prominent. The future of American education rests largely on the actions of the state governments.

In the last few years, the states have done a great deal. This book summarizes some recent changes and considers the future. It begins with a brief review of the context for state action. Although state efforts to improve education were enhanced by the spate of critical reports on America's schools, state activities in this area clearly predate the reform reports. Moreover, the actions that have been taken were heavily influenced by changes in the nature and character of state government that took place over the last two decades. The second section briefly reviews the states' recent efforts to improve the quality of education. We do not try to count the precise number of reforms. Such a task is unnecessarily complex, and the numbers themselves are in a constant state of flux as states continue to revise and reshape their programs. Rather, we describe the range of new initiatives and try to summarize several leading examples of the major reforms. Finally, we discuss a series of long- and short-range concerns that will have a major bearing on the ultimate success, or failure, of the efforts to improve the schools.

2
The Context of Reform:
The Capabilities and Interests
of State Governments

The states' recent efforts to improve the quality of education did not emerge full blown in response to a call for better schools. During the last thirty years, state governments have played an increasingly important role in setting the course of public education and financing it. In 1963, states provided 39 percent of all education revenues; in 1983 they provided 49 percent of the total. Over the same period, the contribution of local governments fell from 56 percent of the total to 44 percent.[1]

Part of the impetus for state reform came from the increased professionalization of state governments, which made it possible for governors and legislators to play a more active role. Expansion was also encouraged by a growing interest in education quality, concern about education finance and equal education opportunity, and a growing perception that public policy could play a decisive role in improving the quality of elementary and secondary education. Each of these developments merits careful examination.

Improving the Machinery of State Government

For most of the twentieth century, states have been regarded as the weak link in American federalism. Scholars have always been somewhat suspicious of them. In 1933, political scientist Luther Gulick wrote: "The American state is finished. I do not predict that the states will go, but affirm that they have gone."[2] In 1965 Roscoe Martin observed: "It is a central conviction of this study . . . that the states have not been able or willing to assume their share of federal responsibilities, particularly during the last three decades, and that the national government has been compelled to develop active relations with local governments in order to make the American system operationally effective."[3]

Scholars were not alone in criticizing the states. Former North Carolina Governor Terry Sanford began his 1967 book *Storm over the States* with the admission:

The states are indecisive.
The states are antiquated.
The states are timid and ineffective.
The states are not willing to face their problems.
The states are not responsive.
The states are not interested in the cities.
These half dozen charges are true about all of the states some of the time and some of the states all of the time.[4]

The states have changed. Their governmental machinery is much more effective and efficient than it was twenty years ago. Reapportionment of state legislatures, constitutional modernization, and administrative reform have altered the face of state governments and have increased their capacity to govern.

The most important changes took place in state legislatures. Following the Supreme Court's one man, one vote decisions, state legislatures were reapportioned to make them more representative.[5] Reapportionment increased the voting strength of cities and suburban areas and decreased the power of rural areas. It also helped produce a different kind of legislator. According to one recent study, "state legislators are now thought to be more intelligent, assertive, independent, diverse in background, and critical of government policy."[6]

In addition to becoming more representative, state legislatures improved their capabilities by modifying constitutional restrictions on authority, length of sessions, compensation, professional staff, and rules and procedures. Limitations on the length of sessions were frequently eliminated or relaxed to allow more time for deliberation. Restrictions on matters to be considered in second sessions were eased. The number of legislative staff members increased sharply. Staff specialization has also increased. Many legislatures have created fiscal, audit, and evaluation units; administrative, research and bill-drafting staffs were also added in many places. In 1980, the National Conference of State Legislatures estimated that there were 16,000 full-time and 9,000 part-time employees of state legislatures.[7]

Perhaps the California legislature, a body with resources and a knowledge base that rival those of the U.S. Congress, best exemplifies these changes. Indeed, because the states do not have responsibility for (or major interest in) national defense, foreign policy, social security, or the federal budget deficit, they can devote their talents and energies to a narrower range of issues. California's leg-

5

islature, for example, meets in a continuing two-year session, and its members and professional staff are well paid. The legislature has a stable of administrative assistants, secretaries, clerks, and district case workers. It has a complete, year-round committee system fully staffed with majority and minority employees. It has a legislative counsel (which drafts bills and provides general legal support), a legislative analyst (a precursor of the Congressional Budget Office), a legislative auditor, and offices of research for both the General Assembly and the Senate. In many respects, it is a smaller version of the U.S. Congress. Indeed, California's legislature may be more competent than the Congress—it does not yet suffer from giantism.

State governors have also changed. According to one recent study, gubernatorial powers have been expanded and strengthened significantly by the use of the executive budget, planning and management tools, and an enlarged veto power. Moreover, like the legislatures, governors' offices are generally bigger and better staffed than they were previously. Governors' staffs have grown from an average of eleven persons in 1956 to thirty-four in 1979.[8]

Like their legislative counterparts, the personal characteristics of governors are also different: The new governors are younger, better educated, and more heterogeneous.[9] Changes in government organization have also been important; between 1965 and 1977, twenty-one states undertook a major reorganization of their executive branch. Similarly, the number of states using a cabinet system increased from ten in 1969 to thirty-five in 1981. Although the powers and responsibilities of state cabinets vary, they almost always serve as a problem-solving group for the governors.[10]

State administrative agencies show similar developments. Administrative procedures and internal management have been improved. The increased activity in state governments has made it easier to attract better-trained and more diverse staff. State agencies are now likely to employ specialists in such areas as planning, finance, research, and evaluation.[11] According to the Census Bureau, between 1954 and 1983 the number of total state employees increased from 1.1 million to 3.8 million, a growth of more than 250 percent. During the same period the number of federal civilian employees grew only slightly, from 2.4 to 2.9 million, or about 20 percent.[12]

Finally, states have made their revenue systems more broadly based and efficient. Income taxes have become a more important source of state revenues, amounting to 37 percent of all collections in 1983. Sales taxes by comparison have declined; in 1983, these taxes accounted for less than half of all state tax revenue, the lowest percentage in fifty years. In 1983, according to the Council of State

Governments, forty-five states had a sales tax, forty-four had individual income tax, and forty-six had corporate income tax.[13]

This impressive evidence does not mean that state governments are now a paradise of government efficiency. The states have always varied in their political and administrative capabilities, and they still do. One recent analysis noted that state governments are often "plagued by fragmentation, disarray, confusion and lack of leadership."[14] The Advisory Commission on Intergovernmental Relations recently concluded that only a few states had developed "broad and comprehensive strategies which can bring state assistance to bear on community problems in coordinated fashion."[15]

Even if they have not solved all their problems, state governments are now much more capable and significant partners in the federal system than they were twenty years ago. Their increased political and administrative capabilities have made it easier for elected state officials to assume a leadership role in all areas of social policy. Because education consumes a large portion of every state's budget, this growing competence made it inevitable that elementary and secondary education would attract the attention of legislators and governors.

The States' Interest in the Quality of Education

Throughout the 1970s, evidence accumulated that American education was in trouble. The most carefully watched barometer was the Scholastic Aptitude Test (SAT). By the early 1970s, it was clear that the SAT scores of the nation's college-bound high school students were steadily declining. The news media gave great attention to the annual release of the scores, much to the consternation of the College Board and the Educational Testing Service.

In 1975 the College Board established the Advisory Panel on the Scholastic Aptitude Test Score Decline, which was chaired by former Labor Secretary Willard Wirtz, to analyze the issue. The panel concluded that the declines were the product of several factors, including the changing composition of students taking the exam, "the dispersal of learning activities and emphasis in the schools," "the diminished seriousness of purpose and attention to the mastering of skills and knowledge in the learning process," "the impact of television," the role of the family in the educational process, and diminution in student motivation.[16] In short, everything was responsible, but nothing was entirely to blame. A rereading of this study today is of substantial interest because the issues it raises were cited again—to much greater effect—by the education reports of the early 1980s.

State legislators and governors, of course, did not need anything as arcane as SAT scores to judge the quality of education and its relative importance to their constituents. Unhappy constituents express their views freely, and only the most obdurate legislators could have been unaware of increasing dissatisfaction. Legislators who wanted a more precise gauge than constituent mail, phone calls, and conversation could study the annual Gallup Poll on Public Attitudes toward Education, conducted by the *Phi Delta Kappan*. For more than a dozen years the public displayed a steadily declining level of confidence in the public schools. One question stands out: the poll's request that the respondents assign a letter grade to the local schools. Between 1974 (when the question was first asked) and 1982, the percentage giving the schools an A or B rating fell from 48 percent to 37 percent. The response of parents with children in the public schools showed a similar drop, from 64 percent in 1974 to 49 percent in 1982. Thus the people likely to be most familiar with the public schools have a higher regard for them than the general public does, but both groups show pronounced declines. Few state legislators and governors read *Phi Delta Kappan*, but the widespread attention that the media gave to the results of the annual poll ensured that elected officials at all levels of government knew the public's feelings about the schools.[17]

The legislators and governors did not necessarily believe the interest groups who argued that there was nothing wrong with schools that more money would not fix. One little-noted but very important aspect of interest group politics is the cynicism it breeds. Legislators and their staffs may bend to the wishes of specific interest groups because of the financial resources they command or the votes they may deliver, but they do so without illusion. They know only too well that interest groups are not entirely motivated by altruism and a selfless pursuit of the public interest. Indeed, the more an interest group claims that its interest is wholly motivated by the urge to beneficence—that it acts "for the good of kids," for example—the more likely the experienced legislator is to dismiss the claim. These interest groups, like others, are thus tarred: they are taken seriously as a political force, but their rhetoric about the public interest is not.

With respect to education policy, many state legislators responded by cutting the ties that had bound them to education interest groups. No longer were superintendents' or teachers' groups viewed as disinterested experts. As a consequence state legislators were progressively more willing to tie funding increases to education reform, as they, and not educators, saw such measures.

One popular response to the decline in the quality of the schools was the "accountability movement," a loose collection of techniques designed to improve both school management and educational outcomes. The techniques often involved quantitative management systems. Thus state governments mandated that the schools employ planning, programming, budgeting systems; management information systems; systems analysis; and planning models. The intention was to use the tools of management science to help the schools pursue educational achievement more efficiently and rationally. "Accountability," however, was a vague term that meant different things to different audiences and soon fell into disfavor.

Another response to the decline in quality was the establishment of minimum competency testing programs for high school students. These programs required students to take and pass a state-designed test, either at specified points during their educational experience or before they completed high school. Education groups frequently opposed these testing programs, but the public approved them, and their popularity spread rapidly. In 1975 no state had these programs; thirty-seven states had them four years later.[18]

The impetus for minimum competency tests came from several sources. In some cases elected officials were the driving force. In other states the chief state school officer or the state board of education played a major role. In a few places educators took the initiative after elected officials passed the word that they would do so if the education establishment did not. The reason for the interest was straightforward: Elected officials usually want to know what they are getting for the public's dollar. Legislators wanted some measure of school outputs, particularly when quality was declining. Despite the concerns about the limits of test scores as indicators of achievement, many politicians pushed ahead.

A longstanding belief that politicians should not interfere with matters best left in the hands of professional educators continued to deter most legislatures from mandating the specifics—what was taught, how it was taught, and who taught it. This fine-grained detail remained the province of local boards and superintendents. But, as the quality of education declined, so too did the willingness of elected officials to let educators have the final word on these matters.

Legislators did deal with a wide range of education issues in the 1970s, however, including finance reform, collective bargaining, desegregation, and textbook selection policy. As always, financing education was a major concern. Between 1970 and 1981, twenty-eight states reformed their systems of school finance.[19] Occasionally they acted under duress: In 1976, for example, the New Jersey Supreme Court closed the state's public schools until the legislature complied with the terms of the Public School Education Act of 1975, a law designed to equalize educational expenditures within the state. Eventually the legislature was forced to impose an income tax to raise revenue for education.[20]

Finance reform was a complicated topic that meant different things in different states, and nuances were important. An expansion in equalization aid to compensate for local property wealth disparities did not necessarily reduce disparities in per pupil expenditures, just as development of new measures of school district fiscal capacity did not necessarily lead to greater attention to programs for special pupil populations or recognition of special characteristics of some districts. Not surprisingly, school finance reform was usually accompanied by greater state expenditures for education.[21] "Leveling down" has never been an attractive reform strategy, and as state legislatures tried to equalize expenditures between poor and wealthy districts, they preferred to raise the poor to the level of the better off rather than the reverse.

Desegregation was another major issue for state policy makers in the 1970s. Many judicial decisions forced the desegregation of metropolitan school districts, often over the strenuous protests of local residents and state government officials. In addition, many states created programs to address the educational needs of minority and disadvantaged students. Although the enactment of these programs was frequently controversial in conservative state legislatures, the efforts to create them were reasonably successful. A 1982 study found that twenty-three states provided funds to local school districts for disadvantaged students; twenty-three states mandated services to students with limited ability to speak English; and all states provided funds to help meet the costs of educating handicapped children.[22]

Finally, state governments were very concerned with the unionization of the teaching force and the need to establish a framework for collective bargaining between teacher unions and local school officials. The growth in teacher unionization was startling. In 1960, the American Federation of Teachers (AFT) represented about 50,000 teachers and the National Education Association (NEA) had some 700,000 members. In 1983 the NEA had a membership of 1.6 million and the AFT more than 600,000. Teacher union officials estimated that about 90 percent of the nation's teachers carried union cards.[23] Many other school personnel belonged to other unions, such as the American Federation of State, County, and Municipal Employees.

Collective bargaining by public employees was a new phenomenon for state legislators, and they found the issues associated with it always complex and often divisive.

Together, these issues were often unpopular. Finance reform sometimes meant taking money from one jurisdiction and giving it to another. Desegregation meant busing and sometimes violence. Few people were happy with the former, and nobody wanted the latter. Collective bargaining too often meant teacher strikes—something unheard of in previous decades. In short, in the 1950s and 1960s education was a popular and generally positive activity for elective officials, but by the 1970s it had lost its luster.

The declining interest in education and the lack of political rewards for state politicians were highlighted in a 1981 survey by the Eagleton Institute of Politics at Rutgers University. The survey found that, for the previous fifteen years, education leadership in state legislatures was usually the product of a "single, unusually committed group of legislators." Education was not a popular area for new legislators because, in the words of one legislator, "there are no goodies to hand out like years ago."[24]

In the case of education, the goodies had never included money. Education committees were not the plum that banking, commerce, or labor had always been. Rather, the goodies were counted in terms of what economists call psychic income, or nonmonetary satisfaction. In the 1960s, California, for example, had education committees in both houses, with chairmen and members of great distinction; no other committees (excepting only Rules) could be so described. For many members, education was their "good government" activity, and the education system was the beneficiary.

The Quality of Education Can Be Improved

Recent research evidence suggesting that the quality of a school could be improved also encouraged state governments to direct more attention to education. Since the mid-1960s educators and policy makers had believed that variations in school quality affected a child's achievement considerably less than did a child's socioeconomic background.

The primary evidence supporting the earlier view was a massive study for the U.S. Office of Education by sociologist James Coleman. The report, formally called *Equality of Educational Opportunity* (and popularly known as the Coleman Report), concluded that educational achievement was related more to the student's family background than to the characteristics of the school (facilities, materials, curricula, teachers, and so on).[25] This landmark study left educators and policy makers deeply shaken. In Diane Ravitch's words:

> The most important point to filter through the public prints was that "schools don't make a difference." If student achievement is determined largely by family background and scarcely at all by teachers, books, and facilities, the reasoning went, then improving the school is unlikely to have much effect on student achievement. This finding raised serious doubts about the likely value of compensatory education for poor children, which was just beginning to burgeon in response to the passage of federal aid to education only the year before.[26]

Other studies by such eminent social scientists as Frederick Mosteller and Daniel P. Moynihan and by Christopher Jencks and his colleagues further supported this interpretation.[27]

By the mid-1970s, however, mounting evidence indicated that school structure and organization had a powerful effect on what a child learned. Ironically, James Coleman was the scholar whose work, done with his colleagues Thomas Hoffer and Sally Kilgore, most conveyed this finding in the United States. Coleman's group concluded that the conditions of educational success were discipline (physical and intellectual), high expectations and standards (for both teachers and students), and a safe and orderly environment. According to their research, these conditions were more likely to be found in private and Catholic schools than in public schools, a conclusion that stimulated great debate and in the process actually diverted attention from the broader lessons.[28]

Other scholars also emphasized the importance of school variables in educational achievement. Indeed, the path-breaking study was not Coleman's but that of an English psychiatrist and his colleagues. In a three-year study of a dozen secondary schools in London, the research team found that "schools do indeed have an important impact on children's development, and it does matter what school a child attends."[29] Team members found that the schools' "ethos" (or atmosphere) made a major difference in student achievement. More specific factors cited included the effective use of classroom time, teacher expectations about student work and behavior, frequent feedback to students about their performance, schoolwide agreement on values and norms, frequent teacher-student interaction, and teachers' attitudes toward students.

Barbara Lerner asserts that four factors (the amount of homework, the class time spent directly on school work, class attendance, and textbook difficulty levels) are the key determinants of achievement; appropriately, she refers to them collectively as "the hard work

12

variable."[30] Sara Lawrence Lightfoot's study *The Good High School* also noted the importance of a school's atmosphere, the leadership provided by principals, the regard for teachers and their work, and the expectations for students.[31]

Further evidence on variables that influence academic performance appears in the growing body of literature on school effectiveness. This research involves a variety of methodologies, with different levels of sophistication and methodological rigor. In general, it focuses on five ingredients: strong administrative leadership (the principal), high expectations for achievement, an orderly learning environment, emphasis on basic skills, and frequent monitoring of pupil progress. One review of this literature concluded that the individual studies were frequently flawed, but that collectively they made sense. Purkey and Smith wrote: "We find it weak in many respects, but most notably in its tendency to present narrow, oft times simplistic recipes for school improvement derived from non-experimental data. Theory and common sense, however, do support many of the findings of school effectiveness research."[32]

Regardless of the methodological shortcomings of the literature, throughout the 1970s, the evidence suggested that the schools were failing their students and the nation. As noted earlier, public opinion polls reflected lower public support for public schools.[33] Articles about the quality of education began to appear in the popular literature.[34]

Education for Economic Growth

By the late 1970s, state interest in education received another boost, this one from the growing perception that high quality education was necessary to ensure economic competitiveness. The belief had two interrelated components. First, that high quality education would help ensure a highly trained and motivated labor force, a necessity in an increasingly technological world. Second, the presence of good schools would attract new industries and would help keep old ones.

The emphasis on education for economic growth was especially popular in the Southeast. Governors Graham of Florida, Robb of Virginia, Winter of Mississippi, Clinton of Arkansas, Hunt of North Carolina, and Alexander of Tennessee took a major personal interest in education. To some extent these states were simply catching up: All of them ranked well below the national average in per pupil education expenditures. But other motivations—political, social, and economic—also led the governors to take action in education. The types of initiatives they launched also varied. Governor Robb, for example, sought to increase teacher salaries, Hunt focused on math

13

and science programs, and Alexander and Clinton addressed teacher knowledge and competence. The governors' stated concern, however, remained the same: the need for high-quality education to ensure the state's economic competitiveness. Their argument was well received by state legislatures and the public alike.

Many states had thus taken actions to improve their schools (or were in the process of doing so) before the recent reform reports were released. Most state legislatures took no fixed attitude regarding what would work and what would not. Policy makers had a straightforward view; they wanted to raise educational standards and to hold educators responsible for the quality of schools. Historically, they had refrained from action because of opposition from the education establishment.

In this environment the National Commission on Excellence in Education was formed. Established in 1981 with little fanfare by U.S. Secretary of Education Terrel Bell, the commission's April 1983 report put education in the headlines. In strong language it described an educational system in chaos:

> The educational foundations of our society are presently being eroded by a rising tide of mediocrity that threatens our very future as a Nation and a people. What was unimaginable a generation ago has begun to occur—others are matching and surpassing our educational attainments. . . . We have, in effect, been committing an act of unthinking, unilateral educational disarmament.[35]

The commission's recommendations called for stronger high school graduation requirements, more rigorous and measurable standards for students, more time spent on instruction, improvements in teacher preparation and compensation, and greater leadership by educators and elected officials. The report touched a sensitive nerve: the day after it was released, the government received more than 400 requests for copies in a single hour. The report also found a receptive audience among federal and state legislators, governors, the media, and the public. The Department of Education estimated that 6 million copies of the report were distributed within a year of its release.

Critical studies of American education with ringing calls for reform are not new. In the last century, major reform-oriented analyses have included the Report of the Committee on Secondary School Studies (1893), better known as the Committee of Ten; *Cardinal Principles of Secondary Education* (1918); *Issues of Secondary Education* (1937); the National Education Association's *Education for All American Youth* (1944); *The American High School Today* (1959); and *Crisis in the Classroom* (1970). The 1970s was an especially active period, with critical reports

14

issued by the National Panel on High Schools and Adolescent Education (1974), the Panel on Youth (1974), the National Commission on the Reform of Secondary Education (1973), the National Task Force for High School Reform (1974), the California Commission for Reform of Intermediate and Secondary Education (1975), and the Carnegie Commission on Higher Education.

Several of these studies had a major impact on American education. James Conant's *The American High School Today*, for example, was published in 1959 shortly after the Russians launched the first space satellite. Conant's call for the creation of comprehensive high schools encouraged states and local school districts to close small schools in the name of economy and educational quality. The book's practical recommendations made it popular with educators and the public alike.[36]

Despite Conant's success and that of a few other studies, most education reform reports age quickly, and the sense of urgency fades. Judging from the long-term effect of these early studies, the nation's capacity for critical analysis of the schools is matched only by a lack of willingness to take strong action to improve them.

The report of the National Excellence Commission, like Conant's effort, was written at a propitious time. The nation's interest in reversing the sluggish economic growth of the 1970s created a climate that eagerly accepted the commission's strong indictment of the schools. Moreover, the commission's report was soon followed by studies from other blue-ribbon commissions that reached equally critical conclusions and heightened the need for action.

The Task Force on Education for Economic Growth, for example, wrote that "our future success as a nation—our national defense, our social stability and well being and our national prosperity—will depend on our ability to improve education and training for millions of individual citizens."[37] Its members asked states to develop plans to upgrade education in the public schools from kindergarten through grade 12, create partnerships for improving education, provide the necessary resources and use them effectively, improve the status of the teaching profession, make the academic experience more intense, and take steps to ensure the quality of education.

The report of the Twentieth Century Fund Task Force on Elementary and Secondary Education Policy focused on federal education policy.[38] The task force noted that state and local governments bore the primary responsibility for the nation's schools, but it emphasized that the federal government had an important role to play in ensuring that schools were of high quality, offered equal access, and assisted students with special needs. With this emphasis, the task force separated itself from the Reagan administration's call for a diminished federal role in education.

The National Science Board's Commission on Precollege Education concentrated on education in mathematics, science, and technology.[39] The commission provided a detailed set of recommendations for improvement. It called for a lasting commitment to quality education for all students; earlier and increased exposure to science, mathematics, and technology; better measurement of student achievement; retraining of current teachers; efforts to attract new teachers; the establishment of exemplary programs; and use of all available resources, including the new information technologies and informal education.

Just when the public's attention was focused on education, several large-scale studies provided greater in-depth analysis of how schools work. John Goodlad's *A Place Called School*[40] was the product of several years labor, as were Theodore Sizer's *Horace's Compromise*[41] and Sara Lawrence Lightfoot's *The Good High School*.[42] All reflected extensive observations of classrooms and sought to show how teachers taught and students learned. All three, however, were primarily research studies, more intent on accurate portrayal and interpretation than on policy prescriptions. Like these three studies, Ernest Boyer's *High School: A Report on Secondary Education in America*[43] was based on a multiyear research project. A small army of consultants and staff visited schools and reviewed research evidence. Unlike Goodlad, Sizer, and Lightfoot, Boyer and his colleagues advanced a comprehensive set of recommendations for correcting the deficiencies they found.[44]

It is important that the quality of the reports and their impact in generating change not be overstated. These studies are not without faults. Most of the commission reports have methodological shortcomings, and they do not always present a complete and balanced picture of the evidence. Paul Peterson, for example, examined six major reform reports and concluded:

> with some exceptions, the studies do not address the most difficult conceptual and political issues. Instead, they reassert what is well-known, make exaggerated claims on flimsy evidence, pontificate on matters about which there could scarcely be agreement, and make recommendations that either cost too much, cannot be implemented, or are too general to have any meaning.[45]

Similarly, Lawrence Stedman and Marshall Smith noted:

> These reports are political documents; the case they make

16

takes the form of a polemic not a reasoned treatise. Rather than carefully marshalling facts to prove their case, they present a litany of charges without examining the veracity of their evidence or its sources. . . . Caveats and detailed analysis of evidence might have lessened the reports' impacts.[46]

In addition, many of the states would have taken steps to improve education even if the reports had not been issued. In some cases, the recently enacted changes had been under consideration for some time. In Florida and California, for example, state action was likely even without the national reports. There is little doubt, however, that the reports encouraged action in these states and put the issue on the public agenda in many others, something that would not otherwise have happened.

Regardless of its origin, the extent of education reform following the release of these reports is startling. According to a July 1984 report by the Education Commission of the States,

to date, more than 250 state task forces have sprung up to study every aspect of education and to recommend changes. Thousands of education bills have been introduced in state legislatures. Teacher certification, high school graduation and postsecondary admissions standards have been raised in many states. Business leaders, community groups and countless individuals who have not customarily been involved in education have joined together in the last year to define and carry out a new agenda for education.[47]

The results of their labors are impressive. Table 1 illustrates the wide range of actions taken in the last year or currently under consideration.

Not only is the action widespread, it is often quite deep. In Arkansas, the legislature passed 122 separate measures concerning the public schools between September 1983 and September 1984.[48] The Texas legislature met in a special session, passed a comprehensive school reform package, and enacted a finance reform bill to pay for it. Florida has enacted so much legislation that the state senate was asked to put a moratorium on new education measures until those already approved had been implemented. South Carolina adopted a series of sweeping education reforms and raised taxes to pay for them.

The very process of measuring reform, however, reveals a pervasive problem: We have only quantitative measures by which to assess a theoretically qualitative change. Unfortunately, the education system has no commonly accepted set of qualitative measures that permit more careful and useful statements about reform. Indeed, that a state passes very many laws tells us little about actual reform, and intense interest itself is no guarantee of results.

TABLE 1

RECENT INITIATIVES REPORTED BY STATES
AND THE DISTRICT OF COLUMBIA

	Under Consideration or Proposed	Enacted or Approved	Total
Increased high school graduation requirements	6	41[a]	47[a]
Higher college admissions standards	11	22	33
New or revised student evaluation/testing	7	37[a]	44[a]
Changes in adoption procedures	9	13	22
Special academic recognition programs	5	25	30
Increased instructional time[b]	14	20[a]	34[a]
Longer school day[b]	11	11[a]	22[a]
Longer school year[b]	12	8[a]	20[a]
State-supported specialized schools	6	14[a]	20[a]
State-supported academic enrichment programs	8	34[a]	42[a]
Improved school discipline policies	8	19	27
State-mandated placement/promotion policies	4	15[a]	19[a]
State academic requirements for extracurricular/athletic participation	8	13	21
Raised teacher preparation/certification standards	14	35	49
Performance-based teacher incentives[c]	15	22[a]	37[a]
Efforts to address teacher shortages	11[a]	26	37[a]
State-sponsored professional development programs for teachers	14	30[a]	44[a]
State-sponsored professional development programs for administrators	12	30[a]	42[a]

a. Includes the District of Columbia.
b. Twenty-seven states have enacted or approved one or more of these three ways to increase instructional time.
c. Of the twenty-two, fourteen (including the District of Columbia) have enacted/approved performance-based incentive plans for implementation or pilot testing. Eight states have a legislative or state board mandate to develop an incentive program.
SOURCE: U.S. Department of Education.

3
Recent Efforts by States to Reform Education

The complexity of the state efforts, and the inevitable differences among them, make it difficult to summarize the work that has been done. Table 1 and other tabulations simply enumerate the number of states enacting reforms. Such tables provide a useful indication of the range of reforms, but they do not give a complete picture. State-by-state summaries, although interesting, do not illustrate the central themes of reform. In this chapter we group the reforms into four basic categories and summarize the action taken by several states. The categories are:

• *Teachers*: career ladders, incentive pay systems, and training/certification measures.

• *The academic experience*: curriculum/graduation requirements, testing, enrichment programs, academic recognition, and minority programs.

• *Financing*: state support, tax increases, changes in funding formulas, and improvements in quality.

• *Organization and structure*: academic calendar, articulation, corporate/school partnerships, and academic bankruptcy.

These categories do not, of course, include all the changes states have enacted, but they do include the most popular types of reform.

Teachers

The recent reports all view teachers as the essential ingredient of successful education. In *Horace's Compromise*, Theodore Sizer calls teachers "the crucial element." He writes: "An imaginative, appropriate curriculum placed in an attractive setting can be unwittingly smothered by journeyman instructors. It will be eviscerated by incompetents. On the other hand, good teachers can inspire powerful learning in adolescents, even under the most difficult circumstances."[1] The reports also conclude that the poor quality of teachers is a major reason for the crisis in education. The National Commission on Excellence, for example, found that the quality of America's teachers had slipped dramatically in recent years. The commission concluded that "not enough of the academically able students are being attracted to teaching; that teacher preparation programs need substantial improvement; that the professional working life of teachers is on the whole unacceptable; and that a shortage of teachers exists in key fields."[2]

Reasons for the deterioration are many. Pay for teachers is not high, even when the short work year is taken into account. The Carnegie Foundation noted that the average starting salaries for teachers with bachelor's degrees in 1981–1982 was $12,769. For engineers with equal education it was $22,368, and for computer scientists, $20,364.[3] Even if teachers worked a full year, as do engineers and computer scientists, the annualized average salary would be less than that paid to other professionals. Perhaps more important than the level of pay is that it is declining in real terms. Between 1971 and 1981, the buying power of teachers' salaries decreased by about 15 percent, even though the average education level and experience of the teaching force increased.[4]

The professional status of teachers has eroded as well. Teachers are often isolated in their classroom, and most have little voice in deciding how their schools are run. They do not select the courses they teach or the books they use. Indeed, the growing importance of curricular specialists has further diminished teachers' professional freedom. Ambitious teachers who hope to "get ahead" are frequently encouraged to become administrators, doubtful advice that robs the schools of many of its most talented teachers.

The supply of available teachers has also diminished as a result of high attrition rates among young teachers, the retirement of older teachers, and the breakdown of employment barriers that previously forced many women and minorities into classrooms because careers in business, law, medicine, and government service were effectively foreclosed. The dwindling supply of teachers, furthermore, coincides with a recent upturn in birthrates that portends increasing numbers of pupils in the near future.

All observers agree that any efforts to reform the schools must pay careful attention to the teaching force. In Sizer's words, "Improving American secondary education absolutely depends on improving the conditions of work and the respect for teachers."[5]

It is not clear, however, exactly how to improve "the conditions of work and respect." Research on teacher motivation suggests that intrinsic rewards are more important motivators than salary.[6] Incentive pay plans themselves may have more negative than positive effects.[7] Despite these difficulties, the states have made extensive efforts to modify the teaching profession. The most frequent changes include career ladders, alternative certification programs, and financial incentives.

Career Ladders. Many states have turned to career ladders to provide incentives for professional mobility and to promote evaluation of people in the teaching force. In Utah, for example, the state authorized a career ladder program and awarded school districts nearly $20 million dollars in flat grants for their efforts. The state Board of Education is responsible for administering the program, but the local school district develops the specific ladder to be used.[8]

South Carolina will also experiment with a career ladder and teacher incentive plans. In 1986–1987, nine school districts will implement different incentive systems, such as career ladders and master teacher and bonus plans. The state Board of Education is currently developing models for these programs. The state will use the pilot program as a basis for selecting models for statewide implementation.[9]

Florida has established a two-tier master teacher program. Under the scheme, teachers qualify as master teachers if they have four years' teaching experience (at least two years of which must have been spent in Florida); a master's degree in an appropriate field, a certificate of vocational training, or a superior score on an examination in the appropriate subject matter; and superior classroom performance as determined by the principal and an outside observer. The plan is limited to some 6,000 public school teachers (about 5 percent of the state's teaching force), who will receive $3,000 bonuses. Those selected may receive the bonus for three years without being reevaluated.[10]

Tennessee has the most comprehensive career teacher plan. The ladder has five rungs. Beginning with a "probationary teacher" rank (a one-year appointment, followed by promotion to the second rung or dismissal), teachers proceed to the apprentice level and eventually to "Career Level III." At this level, teachers can earn bonuses ranging from $3,000 to $7,000, depending upon the length of his or her contract. Teachers on the first three rungs are evaluated at the local level; state evaluations are required for the two highest steps.[11]

California has authorized a mentor teacher program, another approach to improving the status of teachers. Under the California initiative, as many as 5 percent of the teachers in a local school district could be selected as mentor teachers by a committee composed of teachers, administrators, and parents. Mentors, whose responsibilities include curriculum development or assisting beginning teachers, will receive at least $4,000 a year extra for their efforts. More than 80 percent of California's school districts are expected to participate in this optional program.[12]

Teacher Testing and Certification. State mandates to test teacher competence are increasingly popular. According to the American Association of Colleges for Teacher Education, in March 1984 thirty states had such mandates, and twelve other states were planning such requirements.[13]

There is widespread variation in the states' efforts. Tests may address: (1) basic skills such as math, English, and science; (2) professional or pedagogical skills; and (3) academic knowledge of a particular subject matter. Testing may occur before admission to the teacher education program or before certification. Some states have developed and use their own tests; others rely on nationally standardized exams. The source of the mandate for teacher testing also varies: in eleven cases it is state law, whereas in twenty-two others it is state education agency regulations (three states have both).[14]

Alternative approaches to certification are also being developed. California has an alternative certification route available for math and science teachers in secondary schools.[15] Two states—Florida and New Jersey—are considering certification procedures that completely bypass traditional education courses.

The New Jersey plan is especially interesting. Under the proposal local school districts may hire applicants who have baccalaureate degrees, are of good moral character, and have a passing score on tests in the appropriate subject matter. Each candidate will spend twenty to thirty days working in a classroom and attending a seminar on effective teaching, classroom management, and child development. In the program's second phase, the teacher takes a full-time assignment under the guidance of a professional support team (composed of the school administrator, an experienced teacher, a curriculum supervisor, and a college faculty member). The provisional teacher will also attend seminars on such topics as learning theory and student assessment. At the end of the probationary year, the support team evaluates the teacher's potential. The administrator who heads the team makes the final recommendation for certification.[16]

Financial Incentives. States are using a variety of programs to increase teachers' income. Several states have enacted across-the-board salary increases for all teachers. Virginia, for example, has added resources to the state aid program to encourage local school districts to raise all teachers' salaries by 10 percent each year for two years. Mississippi has boosted the pay of all teachers. California and Ohio have encouraged increases in starting pay for beginning teachers.

In most cases, however, reforms in teacher pay programs are tied to performance. Public opinion polls repeatedly demonstrate that the public will support higher salaries if reform is part of the package.[17] Twenty-two states have enacted some type of performance-based teacher incentives, and another fifteen are considering such measures.[18] Many of these enactments and proposals are career ladder programs similar to those described earlier. Twenty-eight states now offer loans (often with cancellation or forgiveness provisions for people who actually teach), scholarships or new training programs to prospective teachers, and several other states have such initiatives pending.[19]

Among the new plans that establish financial incentives for teaching excellence, Florida's is perhaps the most comprehensive. As noted earlier, Florida has a major master teacher/career ladder program. The state also has a comprehensive merit pay program. Under the District Quality Instruction Program, local districts may qualify for state funding for merit pay for teachers. Districts develop plans for awarding bonuses and submit them to the state for approval. Districts may elect to reward all teachers in an outstanding school, teachers whose students make extraordinary gains, or teachers who have particularly difficult assignments or who teach in areas of critical shortage.[20]

Professional Development. Greater professional development opportunities for both teachers and school principals have also proved a popular education reform. According to the Department of Education, by October 1984 thirty states had established such programs for teachers and/or for administrators.[21]

In-service training for teachers has long been a feature of American education. Unfortunately, the level, quality, and usefulness of the sponsored activities have varied considerably. Several states have sought to improve the professionalization of the teaching force by expanding or improving these programs. The type and focus of the new state efforts varies considerably.

Some states, such as Alabama and Michigan, are considering longer contracts to allow teachers more time for professional development. Other states, such as South Carolina, have created centers that provide teachers with opportunities to study advanced topics. A few states have adopted very innovative practices. Alaska, for example, uses satellite communications to bring instructional television and audio conferencing to many rural school districts. Perhaps the most common approach to teachers' professional development is seen in the states that require or urge local school districts to provide greater in-service opportunities and leave the design of the programs to local initiative.[22]

A similar effort, but a greater departure from the status quo, is the establishment of professional development efforts aimed at school administrators. The contribution of effective leadership by school officials, especially principals, to the quality of education is widely recognized. But, in the past, few formal efforts have been made to ensure that school principals were well equipped to carry out their responsibilities.

In recent years, the situation has been changing. Several states established administrator development programs in the late 1970s, including Pennsylvania, Florida, South Carolina, Maryland, and North Carolina. In the last two years, however, many more states have followed their lead, with activities ranging from in-service training to principals' academies. The increasingly popular principals' academies often provide short-term intensive instruction similar to that offered in the management seminars frequently taken by business executives. One such session was recently offered in Arizona, where school principals participated in a ten-day program that emphasized classroom management techniques, evaluation of teachers, and student discipline.[23] It seems likely that such programs—both for teachers and for administrators—will become increasingly popular in the future.

The Academic Experience

There is widespread agreement that the academic experience offered in most American secondary schools has sharply deteriorated in the last decade. The widely discussed decline in SAT scores is often taken as evidence that students are no longer intellectually challenged as they once were. The National Commission on Excellence concluded:

> Secondary school curricula have been homogenized, diluted and diffused to the point that they no longer have a central purpose. In effect, we have a cafeteria-style curriculum in which the appetizers and desserts can easily be mistaken for the main courses. Students have migrated from vocational and college preparatory programs to "general track"

courses in large numbers. The proportion of students taking a general program of study has increased from 12 percent in 1964 to 42 percent in 1979.[24]

Recommendations that the school curriculum be made more intense and that the standards for high school graduation be raised were a common theme of the various study commissions. The Task Force on Education for Economic Growth, for example, urged states and local school systems to establish "firm, explicit and demanding requirements concerning discipline, attendance, homework and grades and other essentials of effective schooling." The task force also called for "energetic efforts to strengthen the curriculum. . . . The goal should be both richer substance and greater motivational power: to eliminate 'soft' non-essential courses; to involve students more enthusiastically in learning, and to encourage mastery of skills beyond the basics."[25]

Many of the reports focused on upgrading the attention given to math and science courses. The Report of the National Science Board's Commission on Precollege Education began with the admission: "Alarming numbers of young Americans are ill-equipped to work in, contribute to and profit from and enjoy our increasingly technological society. Far too many emerge from the Nation's elementary and secondary schools with an inadequate grounding in mathematics, science, and technology."[26] The commission recommended a number of steps to address this problem including "a strong and lasting national commitment" to mathematics, science, and technology for all students, with earlier and increased exposure to these fields.[27] Similarly, the Twentieth Century Fund Task Force recommended that the federal government emphasize programs to develop basic scientific literacy among all citizens and to provide advanced training in science and mathematics for secondary school students.[28]

Several of the reports called on colleges and universities to upgrade their admissions requirements to raise the standards for high school graduation (the National Commission on Excellence, the Carnegie Foundation, and the Task Force on Education for Economic Growth all voiced this conclusion). In Boyer's words, "we found that the single most important activity that could cause overnight change in the high school curriculum would be if colleges announce their standards."[29]

State governments have taken a wide range of steps to improve the educational programs offered to students in math, science, and across the board. The most common changes include raising curriculum/graduation requirements, requiring competency testing, installing or expanding academic enrichment programs, and, in a few cases, establishing programs to enhance minority participation.

Curriculum/Graduation Requirements. Forty states and the District of Columbia have taken action to raise high school graduation requirements.[30] Very often, these changes simply increase the number of units students must have in certain basic subjects to graduate. Georgia, for example, has increased the requirements for high school graduation to twenty-one units.[31] Many other states have also adopted this approach.

In some cases the new state requirements are generic; they may require more science, mathematics, or English, but they do not go beyond general stipulations. In Illinois, for example, new graduation requirements mandate that students have three years of English, two each of mathematics and social studies, one of science, and one of the following: foreign language, fine arts, or vocational education. Students must also have four years of physical education, one-half of health, and two and one-quarter of electives.[32] In contrast, Louisiana has enacted more specific requirements: four units of English; three of mathematics (including two of algebra and one of geometry); three units of science (including both biology and chemistry); two and a-half units of social studies (including American history, civics, and one-half unit of free enterprise); two units of health/physical education; and seven and one-half units of electives.[33]

Some states have coupled these increases with provisions for different types of high school diplomas much like the long-standing Regents diploma in New York State. Virginia, for example, has increased its high school graduation requirements from eighteen to twenty credits, including two units in both math and science and an additional unit in either science or math. An optional advanced studies diploma will be awarded to students who take additional courses in math and science and a foreign language.[34] Similarly, Utah has developed new requirements for high school graduation and, along with Florida, will soon require twenty-four credits for graduation, the highest number in the nation. Utah students can, by taking appropriate course work, pursue degrees in the college-entry cluster; the high-interest cluster; or the technical, vocational job-entry cluster.[35]

California has reinstated the high school graduation requirements that were dropped in 1969. The requirements are modest, however—eleven credits—and fall well below the local requirements

26

in most districts.[36] California has established the Golden State Diploma. This degree will be given to students who take and pass a series of state-developed achievement tests.

Student Testing. As noted earlier, many states required some form of minimum competency testing before the recent efforts to reform education. According to the Education Commission of the States, in July 1984, forty states had such programs.[37] Interest in testing has increased sharply in the last two years. According to the U.S. Department of Education, thirty-seven states have initiated, revised, or expanded statewide student assessment programs since the National Excellence Commission released its report.[38] Some of the testing programs are intended to identify students needing remedial help. In other cases, passage of tests is required for high school graduation or for promotion to higher grade levels.

There are many examples. Arkansas has established a testing program for grades 3, 6, and 8. The eighth-grade test is a promotional gate: Students must pass it to enter high school.[39] South Carolina will require students to pass a basic skills unit examination before receiving a high school diploma.[40] The New York Regents have expanded the proficiency examination required of all students who do not take the Regents Examination by adding science and social studies.[41] New Jersey recently adopted a basic skills test that secondary students must pass to receive a state-endorsed high school diploma.[42]

Academic Recognition. States are also increasing their efforts to recognize outstanding academic achievement. By October 1984, twenty-five states had such programs, and five more were considering them.[43] Although most of these programs award certificates or special diplomas (as do the Virginia, California, and Utah programs discussed above), some also provide financial rewards.

Pennsylvania, for example, is developing an honors test for high school seniors. Those scoring in the top 1 percent will receive a college scholarship, and those over a cutoff score will receive an honors diploma.[44] In Washington State the legislature approved a two-year tuition and fee waiver at state colleges and universities for recipients of the newly established Washington scholars program. The state also created the Washington Vocational Award program, which provides a one-year tuition and fee waiver for recipients. Both programs will involve three students from each of the state's forty-nine legislative districts.[45]

Equity Issues. There are concerns that the emphasis on educational excellence will shortchange minority and disadvantaged students. Although the recent state efforts have not focused on these students, several states have adopted new programs designed to help meet their needs. In Texas the education reform package included an increase in equalization assistance, money that will increase state aid to poorer school districts.[46] The new legislation also establishes a voluntary preschool program for four-year-olds who cannot speak English or who have educational disabilities.[47] New Jersey has begun an "urban initiative" to focus assistance and resources on high-need urban schools. The program has two parts: first, funds to assist all the state's urban districts in areas critical to educational improvement; and second, an effort to help urban districts implement a long-term, comprehensive school renewal plan based on specific objectives.[48] South Carolina has also launched a comprehensive program for students who need remedial help. Four-year-olds with developmental deficiencies may attend half-day child development programs. In addition, remedial instruction will be provided for elementary and secondary students who do not meet the state's minimum basic skills requirements, with extra resources concentrated at the elementary school level.[49] South Carolina's commitment to serving the disadvantaged will cost an estimated $60 million, approximately one-third of the total reform package.

College Admissions Standards. Perhaps more important than state diploma requirements are the entrance criteria at public colleges and universities. In many states, admissions requirements at the flagship universities have become the de facto graduation requirements in many school districts. Raising university requirements thus adds rigor to high school curricula. In contrast, easing the requirements, as was too often done in the 1970s, reduces graduation standards.

Twenty-two states have tightened university entrance requirements.[50] In Missouri, for example, the four campuses of the University of Missouri have set admissions standards higher than the new requirements for high school graduation. The university will require four units of English; three of mathematics (algebra or higher); two of science; two of social studies; and three additional units in foreign language, English, mathematics, science, or social science.[51] In the same vein, the University of North Carolina at Chapel Hill has raised admissions requirements to include two years of a foreign language, one course in a laboratory science, and three years of mathematics.[52]

Increased Financial Support for Education

The costs of reforming the schools received only modest attention in most of the education reports. The National Commission on Excellence made no mention of the bill for its reforms, merely noting: "We also call upon citizens to provide the financial support necessary to accomplish these purposes. Excellence costs. But in the long run mediocrity costs far more."[53] The Twentieth Century Fund also failed to estimate the costs of its proposals, simply observing: "The Task Force is aware that some of its proposals are costly."[54] The Task Force on Education for Economic Growth called on states and local governments to "marshal the resources that are essential for improving the public schools," but trod softly on the issue of cost and sources of funds.[55]

Perhaps the most comprehensive program for improving the schools was offered in Ernest Boyer's *High School*, but Boyer did not estimate costs. His book does imply that, if Americans spent less for beauty aids, pet food, and national defense, more money could be spent on education.[56] Indeed, only the report by the National Science Board's Commission on Precollege Education attempted to determine what its recommendations would cost and who should pay for them. The recommendations for federal action alone totaled more than $1.5 billion.[57]

Policy makers do not have the luxury of treating costs so lightly. Improving education will, sooner or later, cost more money. Some reforms would cost more than others. A 20 percent increase in teacher salaries, for example, would cost about $12 billion. Lengthening the school day or lengthening the school year to 220 days in all states, as suggested by the National Excellence Commission, would run about $20 billion.[58] Still, despite the high costs, some states have taken steps to increase or revise education funding. Tax increases, new school finance formulas, and completely new mechanisms for education support have all appeared in the last year.

Tax Increases. Tax increases afford perhaps the greatest indication of the states' willingness to support more spending on education. According to the Task Force on Education for Economic Growth, fifteen states have passed or are considering increases in state sales or income taxes to help fund education.[59]

Several states have increased sales taxes to help finance educational improvements. Arkansas raised the state sales tax from 3 to 4 percent to raise an estimated $154 million in revenue. Local school districts in the state are required to raise their property tax rates to the statewide average and are also required to bring teacher salaries closer to regional averages.[60] Similarly, South Carolina raised its sales tax from 4 to 5 percent to raise some $200 million for education. State sales tax increases have also been enacted (or made permanent) in Utah, Tennessee, Texas, Oklahoma, and Iowa.[61]

Florida will pay for its education reforms through a 1982 increase in the sales tax and a permanent hike in the state's corporate tax rate.[62] Kentucky took several steps to give school districts more revenue options. In 1984 the legislature enacted a law allowing districts to levy a utility gross receipts tax, an excise tax on income, an occupational license tax, or any combination of these taxes. The state also established a minimum property tax level for all districts and exempted the measure from public hearing and recall.[63]

Reforming School Finance. Several states have coupled education reform with revisions of their school finance formula. Odden and Dougherty studied eight states in 1984 and found that two (Arkansas and Texas) had made comprehensive changes in their school finance formulas. In Arkansas, the state moved from a total-dollar save harmless finance plan to a pupil-weighted foundation program that will require property tax increases in nearly one-third of all school districts. The new Texas funding formula relies on a basic grant system adjusted by several factors, including regional cost differences and weighted special programs. The formula will direct more resources (an average of $730 per pupil) to the poorest school districts.

Odden and Dougherty also found that another state (Illinois) will consider major revisions in 1985. Five additional states (California, Florida, South Carolina, Tennessee, and Utah) made more modest changes in their school finance formulas that were designed to increase or assure educational equity.[64]

New Mechanisms. Several new mechanisms to support education are gaining in popularity. One approach—charging students a modest fee for extracurricular activities such as band and sports—was widely initiated in California following the enactment of Proposition 13. The fee system is also popular in Utah and Wisconsin. In April 1984 the California Supreme Court ruled that extracurricular activities were "educational in character," and concluded that public school officials may not charge participants fees. Although this decision prevents California schools from using the system, it does not of course apply directly to other states, nor does it mean that other services, such as preschool or child care programs, may not be offered on a fee basis.[65]

State and local education foundations have also been launched to raise funds from nongovernmental sources. In November 1982 West Virginia launched the West Virginia Education Fund to support "innovation and creativity" in the public schools. Several other states, including Arizona and Kentucky, have already launched similar foundations, and other states are investigating the concept.[66] According to the Task Force on Education for Economic Growth, more than 200 local education foundations have been started.[67]

Another development bears watching. In November 1984 California voters approved Proposition 37 by a substantial margin (58 percent to 42 percent), establishing a state lottery. Exactly one-half of the proceeds are to be spent on prizes, 10 to 16 percent on administration, and the balance—34 to 40 percent—is earmarked for education. Supporters of the measure have claimed it will raise nearly $700 million a year for education. Education groups were divided on the proposition, with the Parent-Teacher Association opposed and the California Teachers Association in favor.[68]

The Business Community and the Schools. The most far-reaching new initiative in education to emerge in recent years is the growing corporate interest in the public schools. Although the private sector has traditionally played a key role, business involvement began to diminish about twenty years ago when the education policy agenda— civil rights, school finance, and collective bargaining—became increasingly bitter and confrontational. Today, however, the business community is again turning to the public schools.

Several factors have encouraged corporate interest. First, the growth of a global economy has created the need for a better educated, more highly trained, more productive work force. Second, the shift in our economic base toward information and technology-based industries has created a demand for entry-level employees with good skills in communications, science, mathematics, and technology. Finally, businesses derive public relations benefits, both internally and externally, from close working relationships with the public schools.

The types of activities that corporations sponsor vary considerably. In some cases, corporate ventures support the status quo in the schools. In other cases business involvement may underwrite modest innovation or incremental changes. In a few cases, the business community may sponsor activities that aim to make fundamental changes in the public schools.

The range of corporate-sponsored activities is as broad as corporate imaginations. In many cases, individual corporations launch specific education-related projects. The Bank of Boston created a $1.5 million permanent endowment fund to award grants to local educators to devise ways to improve the quality of teaching.[69] The GTE Corporation has established a teacher fellowship program for outstanding math and science teachers. Some 1,000 businesses in the Dallas area participate in that region's Adopt-A-School program.[70] IBM donated 2,000 personal computers to 130 public schools as part of a program to train teachers and students to use the machines.[71]

State governments are encouraging such cooperative ventures: California recently authorized a special tax break for companies that donate computers to schools. Similarly, Idaho recently authorized state income tax deductions for donations of equipment and materials to schools and libraries.[72]

In other places the business community has sponsored consortia arrangements that involve a number of different organizations. The Project to Improve Math Mastery in Connecticut, for example, involves schools, postsecondary institutions, and the corporate community in an effort to improve the teaching of mathematics in the public schools. The Philadelphia Alliance for Teaching Humanities in the Schools seeks to develop a model for improving humanities instruction in an urban high school. It is a joint effort of the business community, higher education, and the Philadelphia public schools and is supported by both public and private sources.

The private sector has also sought to improve the management of the public schools in some areas. In New York, the Economic Development Corporation lends business personnel to the schools. Similarly, a task force of Chicago business executives undertook a four-month analysis of the Chicago public schools. In Minneapolis the corporate community supported a long-term strategic planning process for the public schools.

Finally, in at least two cases, the business community has sought major structural changes in state education policy as a way of improving the schools. The California Business Roundtable conducted a major study of the state's public schools. After assessing the condition of the schools, the roundtable proposed increased education funding in exchange for major changes in education policy: higher standards and requirements for graduation, strengthened attendance and discipline laws, and a longer school day and year. Similarly, the Minnesota Business Partnership has recommended a set of wide-ranging structural reforms in the public schools. It proposed institutionalizing mastery learning and a statewide voucher system that would allow eleventh- and twelfth-grade students to enroll in alternative education programs offered by schools, higher education institutions, or private industry.

This brief summary is intended to be illustrative. It does not do justice to the wide range of new initiatives that have tied the schools and the business community together, but it does suggest the range and types of business-school partnerships that have been put in place. More significant than any individual action, however, is that the corporate community has committed itself to improving the quality of the public schools. In so doing it has created a potentially powerful influence on the nature and character of American education.

Education Organization and Structure

The education reports were critical of school structure and organization. The National Commission on Excellence noted that, "compared to other nations, American students spend much less time on school work . . ., [and] time spent in the classroom and on homework is often used ineffectively."[73] The commission recommended more homework, better classroom management and organization of the school day, reduced administrative burdens on teachers, and better placement and grouping of students.[74]

Ernest Boyer's study *High School* was critical of the myriad interruptions with which teachers (and students) must contend:

> In a large number of schools, a steady stream of assemblies, announcements, pep rallies, and other nonacademic activities take up precious time, leaving teachers frustrated. At one school we visited, a class was interrupted on three separate occasions by trivial announcements. We agree with the teacher who said . . . "the first step in improving the American high school is to unplug the PA system."[75]

In the same vein the Task Force on Education for Economic Growth urged state governments to increase the "intensity of academic learning time" in the schools. It noted:

> Where nonessential and peripheral courses have invaded the curriculum, school systems must have the courage to put new emphasis on core academic subjects and must devote more time to them. . . . Class sizes must be limited. Teachers must be freed from trivial demands and allowed to teach. Schools should examine each school year . . . to ensure that time is not wasted.[76]

Although more productive use of existing class time was a com-

33

mon theme in the education reports, so was interest in a longer school day and school year. Several observers have noted that other nations, especially Japan, have a 220- or 240-day academic year. Most American schools, in contrast, remain tied to the 180-day year, a legacy of the days when agriculture was the nation's dominant industry and children spent their summers working in the fields.[77]

The National Science Board's Commission urged more time on task in mathematics, science, and technology education.[78] The Task Force on Education for Economic Growth echoed the theme:

> States and local school systems should also consider lengthening the school year and the school day and extending teachers' contracts. Learning time should be increased, moreover, by establishing a wider range of learning opportunities beyond the normal school day and school year: summer institutes and after-school enrichment programs sponsored by business, for example.[79]

All such proposals have been favorably received by state officials. In the last year many states have taken steps to revise the school calendar, restructure state decision making, provide academic enrichment programs, and raise college admissions standards.

Academic Calendar. Many states have mandated changes in the academic calendar. The usual assumption is that more is better. Twenty-seven states have recently initiated new regulations dealing with instructional time, for example instituting longer school days, a longer school year, or policies to increase the number of hours in the school day actually spent on instruction.[80]

Effective July 1984, the average minimum number of pupil-teacher contact days for all states was 178 days, with a range from 173 (North Dakota) to 180 (twenty-six states).[81] Some states are considering modest increases in the school year, but none of these changes would raise attendance to the 220-day level suggested by the National Excellence Commission. In Michigan, for example, the state legislature lengthened the school year from 180 to 200 days, with 190 of the days used for instruction and the balance for teachers' record keeping and professional development.[82] California has chosen to leave the option with local officials. School districts may increase the school year by five days (to a total school year of 180 days). State per pupil payments will finance this extension.[83]

New Jersey has shown that it considers the number of instructional days a serious matter. In July 1983, the commissioner of education filed show cause orders against thirty-five school districts that held graduation exercises before completing 180 days of instruction. Eventually, fourteen districts were fined $2,545 for each day of noncompliance.[84]

Several states have elected to lengthen the school day. Arkansas, for example, went from five to five and one-half hours. Indiana mandated five hours of instruction time for grades K–6 and six hours for grades 7–12, and Louisiana has increased the school day to six hours for all students.[85] Other states are asking for better use of the school day. In Kansas, for example, the governor has called upon schools to make efficient use of instructional time and has urged parents to be aware of how their children use school time.[86] The Alabama state Board of Education has recommended that disruptions of instructional time for noneducational reasons (such as selling magazines and announcements) be limited and has urged that teachers be given planning time, with restrictions on their noninstructional duties, such as monitoring halls.[87]

At least two states are experimentally lengthening both the school day and the school year. In 1983 North Carolina began a three-year pilot program in Polk and Halifax counties. Children in these districts attended school thirty minutes more each day and for ten months instead of nine. Teachers worked for eleven months instead of ten.[88] The state provided $2 million in additional funds per year to support this program. In 1985, however, Polk county withdrew from the project because of community opposition. Some local residents were angered because the program had been launched without public consultation, and others opposed the way in which the extra time was used.[89] In a similar experiment, Utah's Weber and Washington school districts are testing the effects of a longer school day, increased class size, and increased pay for teachers on the basis of student performance.[90]

Academic Bankruptcy. Four states—Arkansas, Kentucky, South Carolina, and Texas—have developed "academic bankruptcy" policies that give the state authority to guarantee educational quality in local school districts. In Arkansas, for example, school districts in which more than 15 percent of the students score below the state-mandated minimum on basic competency tests will face loss of accreditation if they do not demonstrate progress within two years' time. It is anticipated that some school districts will not be able to meet the state standards. A commission is currently developing reorganization plans under which such districts will merge with adjacent districts in order to comply with the state's requirements. In some cases, school districts may form cooperatives with other districts and may use outside personnel and facilities to meet the state's standards.[91]

In Kentucky, school districts whose students fail to meet state-established achievement levels on basic skills tests will receive state assistance to implement a program to improve their performance. The state may require districts to reallocate their funds to address specific program and service needs. If the district fails to implement the improvement plan, the state may limit the district's authority to spend money, may hire or fire personnel, and may modify the school calendar.[92]

State Board. In a unique action, Texas abolished its twenty-seven-member elected state Board of Education until January 1989 and replaced it with an appointed board of fifteen members. When elections resume, the members will come from each of the fifteen new Board of Education districts, but the governor will retain the power to appoint the chair. The law also established a new legislative education board, composed of the leaders of the legislature. This committee will review all education initiatives placed before the Texas legislature. In view of the political power wielded by the committee's members, its approval will be a valuable asset for the state's education legislation. These changes have been approved by the U.S. Department of Justice, which has jurisdiction over changes in the electoral process in Texas under the Voting Rights Act.[93]

Academic Enrichment. Thirty-four states have approved academic enrichment programs in the last eighteen months, and another eight states are considering them.[94] Many enrichment programs are summer institutes for gifted and talented students. In Mississippi, these programs are offered for high school students at Jackson State University and the University of Southern Mississippi.[95] West Virginia has established the Governor's Honor Academy, a four-week summer camp for students gifted in the humanities, fine arts, mathematics, and science.[96] In some cases, residential high schools have been established. In North Carolina, for instance, the state supports the North Carolina School of Science and Mathematics in Durham, a residential program enrolling about 600 gifted students in grades 10 to 12. In 1983, Louisiana opened the School for Math, Science, and the Arts, a four-year residential high school.

In the most ambitious plan for a merit school program, the Florida legislature has enacted a plan to allocate $20 million to school districts for improvements. Half of this sum goes to the 25 percent of each district's schools that have been recognized as "meritorious." The remainder is used to provide incentives for improvement in schools not so designated. The state selects meritorious schools on the basis of several criteria, including student test scores. Negotiations between teacher unions and local school boards determine how the funds are actually spent, although the legislation does stipulate that the money can be used only for programs that promote student achievement and reward teachers financially. As of October 1984, about half of the state's sixty-seven school districts had not submitted plans for the program. Most of these schools' districts have teachers' unions affiliated with the National Education Association, which opposes the concept. Most of the participating school districts have teacher unions affiliated with the American Federation of Teachers, which supports the proposal.[97]

Federal Initiatives

The extensive action by state governments is all the more impressive in view of the absence of an explicit federal response to the call for reform. Following the release of the National Excellence Commission's report, President Reagan said that his administration would continue to work for passage of tuition tax credits, vouchers, educational savings accounts, school prayer, and elimination of the Department of Education.[98] The president made a number of speeches about education, and Congress held extensive hearings, many of which provided a forum for attacking the Reagan administration's proposals for cuts in the education budget.

Despite the rhetoric there were no major federal initiatives. Congress did enact the Carl D. Perkins Scholarship Program, which authorizes scholarships for "outstanding" high school graduates who intend to pursue teaching careers. At the same time Congress created the National Talented Teacher Fellowship Program, which authorized one fellowship for each congressional district to enable experienced teachers to have sabbaticals for study or research, to develop special programs, or to support model teacher programs or staff development. Congress also approved the Mathematics and Science Education Improvement Act (P.L. 93–377), which was designed to improve math and science education. The measure authorizes some $1 billion in expenditures during the next two years, but only $100 million was actually appropriated for 1985.

The federal government did substantially increase education spending in fiscal year 1985. The Department of Education appropriation of $17.9 billion is some $2.5 billion above both the 1984 appropriation and the president's 1985 budget request. The increase does not by itself, however, reveal a pressing desire to reform elementary and secondary education. Nearly half the increase was assigned to the higher education student assistance programs, and the remainder was distributed across the other major education programs, including Chapter I, special education and impact aid. In short, it was an election year budget that provided more money for education spending generally.

In view of the 1985 spending increase, the lack of more substantial federal action cannot be attributed solely to the deficit. Rather, the modest federal activity is in part the result of an inability to conceptualize an appropriate and meaningful response. That inability, coupled with the overwhelming efforts at the state level, probably accounts for the lack of more concrete federal intiatives. But the states have clearly seized the initiative in education reform, and it is at this level that the battle will be won or lost.

4
The Next Phase: Implementing the Reforms

The jury is out on the states' reform efforts and will be for several years. Although much has happened, it is by no means certain that the states, local school districts, and schools themselves will be able to digest all of the reforms that have been approved. Moreover, given the impressive flurry of activity, there is probably a natural tendency, as Senator George Aiken allegedly remarked with respect to Vietnam, to "say we won and bring the boys home." The possibilities for doing exactly this should not be discounted. The 1984 Gallup poll of public attitudes toward education revealed that the public held the schools in higher esteem than at any point in the last decade, implying that recent public action has boosted the standing of the schools, whether or not any improvements have actually occurred.[1]

Short-Term Issues

The future of the reform movement involves a number of variables that are only dimly visible at present. A dramatic technological advance by our allies or foreign competitors, for example, might spur further calls for changes in education policy. In the absence of such high drama, several factors seem especially important for the short-term future of education reform. These considerations—implementing the new reforms, paying for them, measuring whether they have succeeded, and meeting the needs of all students—are the issues to which state officials will now turn their attention.

Administration. The administrative tasks that remain in the wake of the reforms already authorized (and those that will come in the future) are staggering. Colorado has enacted 114 new education laws, for example, and they will require between thirty-five and forty new sets of regulations.[2] Arkansas has enacted 122 new laws.[3] In some states the rush to enact new measures was so furious that the laws may have been less carefully drafted than necessary to ensure smooth implementation.

At the local level there are other problems. The new reforms were sometimes enacted over the fervent opposition of local school officials, school board members, and teachers, the very people who will now be charged with implementation. Some school boards have begun to complain that the new standards were enacted "from the top down." If the reforms prove to be unpopular, they may languish in the absence of a commitment to implement them.[4] According to former Secretary of Education Terrel Bell, such problems are so great that "we face the biggest test of educational leadership, administrative competence and school diplomacy in our history"[5]—a tall order for a set of institutions whose skills in these areas have not been notable in the past.

The process of implementing the new laws seems likely to shift the balance of power even further from local education agencies to state governments. This is not a new development. During the past fifteen years, state governments have played an increasingly visible role in shaping education policy, often at the expense of local school districts. Many of the recent enactments involve two general characteristics that will exacerbate such shifts. First, the reforms envision much more state homogenization and regulation of public school norms, standards, and procedures. Second, the new measures usually include substantially increased education spending by state governments. In some cases, the increased state expenditures will lead to larger state education agencies. Tennessee, for example, has expanded the state department of education to help cope with the administrative demands created by the master teacher plan. These reforms do not necessarily alter the formal organization of public education, but they may well leave less to the discretion of local officials. In tightening control, they invariably narrow the scope of local sovereignty and enlarge the domain of state regulation.

A recent article on the shifting balance between state and local governments in setting education policy noted that the recent education reforms would further alter the state-local balance:

> If the reform pace is maintained at the state level . . ., the results may or may not include more children acquiring more knowledge, but they will definitely include a marked increase in state regulation, direct state administration, and elaborate statewide monitoring and accountability systems, together with a continuing rise in state education spending. As these structures are created and funds are appropriated, the governors and legislators will become less likely—indeed, less able—to lose interest, to relax their grip, or to allow a resurgence of localism. Public elementary and sec-

ondary education already consumes approximately 35 percent of the average state budget, and the education department is frequently the largest and costliest branch of state government. As it gets still larger and more expensive, we are ever less likely to see a revival either of significant local sovereignty or of the ostensibly nonpolitical "lay board-professional staff" governance structure that has characterized most statewide education policy-making. It is already common for governors to have education policy advisors, on their staffs and in their cabinets, who are at least as influential as any "chief state school officer"—the senior professional who heads the state education department under the aegis of a board of regents or state board of education. One also finds more education policy specialists on the staffs of state legislatures, state budget offices, and the like.[6]

It is not hard to find specific examples of laws that will erode the local position by strengthening the hand of state officials. The academic bankruptcy laws, for example, give state governments considerable authority over local school districts. Some Arkansas officials believe that small, rural school districts may be forced to consolidate with adjacent systems as a result of that state's new laws. Florida's requirement that high school students write a paper every week of the school year is a significant intrusion on local authority. The efforts in some states to define, often in painstaking detail, statewide curriculum objectives that schools must meet will also weaken the local hold on the curriculum. State-directed reforms that determine who teaches and what and how teachers are paid will have the same effect.

In short, the role of local officials in education is likely to diminish and that of the state will increase. James Guthrie, formerly chairman of the Berkeley California School Board, observed, "the local school board member is becoming the snail darter of education." There is much truth in his observation, which is particularly ironic in light of recent research findings that educational excellence greatly depends upon characteristics of school districts and individual schools. Regardless of how practical realities compare with research findings, states are assuming more authority for education quality and will have greater responsibilities as well. Once states go down this road it will be very hard to step aside or to back away.

Financing the Reforms. As noted earlier, education reform will cost money, often a great deal of it. Longer school days (or school years), higher teacher salaries, merit pay (or master teachers), and smaller classes will all require additional resources. Although there is some truth to the claim that reform can be accomplished by using current resources more efficiently, public policy is not a zero-sum game. Literal reallocation of resources from one function to another rarely happens; new resources are found, not simply redeployed.

States have already recognized the need for more money. Some states have already increased taxes to meet the costs of reform. In several other cases states have revised their financing formulas to help ensure that money goes to the neediest school districts.

There is often a quid pro quo at work here. Increased school funding is often accompanied by stiffer education standards for students and teachers. Political leaders have often been unwilling to pay more for the same educational results. Educators, for their part, have been willing to accept new standards as the price of increased public support. In Chester E. Finn's words: "The public agrees with the reformers, if some powerful opinion poll data are to be believed. It will dig deeper to pay for markedly better education, but it seems no longer to believe educators who insist that spending more on the current system will produce more learning."[7]

Even if the public and their legislators "dig deeper" to finance reform now, however, it is by no means certain that they will do so indefinitely. Simply too many variables could change. First, despite efforts to broaden their revenue base, state government finances remain vulnerable to broader economic and political developments. The continuing reliance on the sales tax means that a national recession could play havoc with state revenues, much as all previous recessions have done. At the same time, an economic downturn would increase the need for social welfare expenditures such as unemployment insurance and health care. In short, a recession would put state budgets in a vise and squeeze them unmercifully.

A second potential problem is that state budgets are often at the mercy of changes in federal policy. Substantial budget cuts to reduce the federal deficit could create funding pressures at the state level. This is obviously true for changes in social programs, but even reductions in defense spending could increase state unemployment and job training expenditures. Even the current fiscal health of the states may cause future problems with federal policy. Some federal officials believe that state and local governments are in good fiscal health; a study currently under way at the Treasury Department projects a $60 billion surplus by 1989. State officials contend that the Treasury estimates conceal wide variations in the financial conditions of the states, but many observers believe that this apparent evidence

42

of fiscal well-being will be used as a rationale for proposing large budget cuts in programs to state and local governments.[8]

Changes in federal tax policy may also cause problems. The imposition of a flat tax program such as those envisioned by Bradley-Gephardt, Kemp-Kasten, and the Treasury Department would reduce the yield to investors on tax-exempt bonds issued by state and local governments. If the yield does decline, bond issuers such as state governments and agencies will probably have to increase their interest rates to attract investors. This expensive proposition would drain resources from other activities.

A third uncertainty is the movement to limit taxes; a rekindling of the tax cut fervor of the late 1970s could have a major impact on state education spending. Some observers believe that the decisive rejection of citizen-sponsored tax reduction proposals in California, Michigan, Oregon, and Nevada in the 1984 election was the death knell of the tax revolt. Others, however, believe that the tax limitation movement is far from over, noting that Walter Mondale's call for higher taxes was one of the major factors contributing to his defeat. Moreover, the new Populist Conservative Tax Coalition has been started to press for further tax reductions at the state level.[9] The future of the tax limitation movement is unclear, but politicians will probably err on the safe side.

A fourth uncertainty facing the states is the continuing efforts to revise school finance formulas. These efforts, which have received little publicity since the New York Court of Appeals refused to find that state's finance system unconstitutional, are again looming on the horizon. Indeed, some of the earliest school finance cases will soon be revisited: *Robinson* v. *Cahill* in New Jersey (now *Abbott* v. *Burke*), *Rodriguez* v. *San Antonio* in Texas (now *Edgewood Independent School District et al.* v. *Bynum*), and *Horton* v. *Meskill* in Connecticut.[10] Several new finance cases will soon reach the trial stage, including *Kukor* v. *Grover* in Wisconsin, *Webby* v. *King* in Massachusetts, and *Jesseman* v. *State of New Hampshire*. These cases have major financial implications for the states involved.

Given the possible pressures on state and local finances, it is not surprising that new sources of funding for the schools are being eagerly sought. The revenue potential of these sources, however, remains to be determined. The development of state and local education foundations to sponsor innovative activities holds great promise for small strategic grants, but these are not likely to become sizable enough to be a source of major education funding. Fee for service activities are eminently sensible, especially for ancillary services such as preschool, but there is public opposition to the concept for basic education programs, and in some states like California they are unconstitutional. There is great interest on both sides in increased corporate support for the schools. Furthermore, most of the new programs have proved very popular. These programs are very small, however, and will never provide more than a tiny fraction of the resources needed to run the schools. Finally, as noted earlier, in November 1984 California voters approved a state lottery with a proviso that a substantial share of the proceeds be spent on education funding. It remains to be seen whether this innovation will add as much money to state education spending as promised and whether the technique will be adopted in other states.

The controversy that surrounds the complex matter of education finance was apparent in the recent effort to raise teachers' salaries in Mississippi. In 1982 the state received nationwide attention when it enacted a comprehensive education reform package. The need for reform was not seriously disputed. Mississippi did not have state-supported kindergarten or a compulsory attendance law. The state's per pupil education expenditures were the lowest in the nation, and its teachers' average salaries also ranked near the bottom.

In 1985 the state legislature approved a three-year $4,400 pay raise for teachers, but Governor William A. Allain vetoed the bill, arguing that the state could not afford the expense without a tax increase. The legislature promptly overrode the veto. A variety of tax increases will pay for the pay hike, estimated to cost $77 million. Whether the bitterness created in this case will weaken the state's resolve to carry out other parts of the 1982 reform package not yet implemented remains to be seen. Some observers believe, however, that this year's tax increase may undermine next year's startup of a statewide kindergarten program, an expensive reform that will require substantial resources. Regardless of the eventual outcome in Mississippi, complexities and controversies such as these are likely in other states in the coming years.

Equity. A related issue concerns the impact of efforts to improve school quality on equal educational opportunity. Equity has been a principal objective (perhaps *the* principal objective) of federal, state, and local education policy for the last two decades. Many programs have sought to improve minority access to and performance in the classroom. At least some evidence suggests that these efforts have been successful.[11]

The goal of education reform today, however, is excellence not necessarily fairness and access. The new emphasis may not mesh with the equity concerns, and some observers believe it will be detrimental to those who cannot meet the stiffer requirements. The high school attrition rate was 22.8 percent in 1972 but rose to 27.1 percent in 1982, according to the U.S. Department of Education. Although increased high school dropout rates moved in tandem with lower academic standards, the drive toward higher standards may exacerbate this trend.[12]

Illustrations of the problem are not hard to find. Philadelphia's public schools recently tried, for example, to eliminate the social promotion policy that provided automatic grade advances for most elementary school students. The schools designed a new policy requiring students to read and compute at grade level before promotion. But when the schools discovered that some 40 percent of Philadelphia students would not be able to achieve that level, they delayed implementation of the new policy.[13]

A recent report by a coalition of child advocacy groups warned that "at risk" children have largely been ignored in the rush to reform education. The report, entitled *Barriers to Excellence: Our Children at Risk*, said, "Policymakers at many different levels talk of bringing excellence to schools and ignore the fact that hundreds of thousands of youngsters are not receiving even minimal educational opportunities guaranteed under law." Its recommendations included continued attention to the rights of the disadvantaged, more democratic governance of the schools, the establishment of comprehensive early childhood education and day care programs, and the enactment of more equitable and adequate systems for financing schools.[14]

Another recent study suggests that "the new equity agenda" (one that includes both excellence and equity concerns) raises four separate issues: the differential impact of higher standards and tougher requirements; differential access to new curricula and better teaching; differential access to master teachers; and differential access to computers.[15] These issues are very specific to individual sites: Great variation is easily possible within the same school district. Measuring these elements, and taking steps to ensure equitable treatment, is likely to prove more challenging than the equity initiatives of the 1960s and 1970s.

Some advocates of educational reform dismiss such concerns as evidence of a lack of commitment to higher standards for all students.[16] The basing of standards on a student's race would undoubtedly be a blatant form of racism. Still, there is no doubt that high rates of failure for children of any race are more than just an education problem. They are a political problem. Witness, for example, the outcry that accompanied the first administration of Florida's minimum competency test when more than half of the minority students failed.

Florida's response is instructive. The state launched extensive remedial programs to improve student performance. The percentage of minority students who pass the test has increased sharply, although it still lags behind the pass rate for nonminority students (in 1983, 99.5 percent of the blacks passed the communication part of the test and 91 percent passed the mathematics part). Despite the difference, in May 1984, the Eleventh U.S. Circuit Court of Appeals upheld the test, ruling that the results were not racially discriminatory.[17]

Florida's approach—with a heavy commitment to remedial programs and additional assistance—is admirable and is likely to be required in other states to ensure that minority and disadvantaged students are not left behind. Such an approach, however, will require both a long-term commitment and substantial resources.

It is too early to determine how states and local schools will handle the equity issues as they relate to the reforms that address education quality. At present there is both good and bad news. On the positive side, a sizable percentage of the new state education aid is being distributed through state equalization formulas, so that the poorest school districts will receive comparatively more money than wealthy districts. In the same vein, state categorical programs for populations with special needs appear to have been maintained. Finally, a few states have taken steps to ensure that new remediation programs are provided for students who need them. South Carolina's comprehensive remedial program, for all students at each grade who do not meet minimum performance standards, is perhaps the best example.

On the other hand, some new programs, especially career ladder plans for teachers, are flat grants. In these cases, states are distributing the funds on an unequalized basis. Similarly, in other places the states have called for higher standards but require the local school districts to make provision for remedial services. It remains to be seen whether the local schools have the commitment and resources to do so.

Equity considerations have frequently been glossed over in the drive to improve education. When the new laws are implemented and the results begin to filter in, the issue will assume greater importance. The states' handling of this vexing problem may well determine whether the reforms achieve their goal of improving education quality for all students.

Measuring Progress. Yet another immediate problem is measuring improvement in the schools. Progress must be demonstrated. Sooner or later the public and its elected representatives will (and should) want to see a return on their investment. What type of return should be expected? And how soon?

The first question is the more complex. For better or worse, we measure educational progress by student scores on standardized tests. The most popular indicator is the Scholastic Aptitude Test, a measure whose appropriateness for this purpose is disputed.[18] The SAT's beauty is, unfortunately, its simplicity. Two numbers. Up or down. The SAT does not require much interpretation and fits nicely into newspaper headlines. Even the results of the American College Testing (ACT) Program do not receive much attention, in part because they involve a series of five numbers rather than two.

The SAT scores have been moving upward in recent years, and it is not surprising that the public feels better about the public schools, at least for the present. Few educators, however, would want to pin hopes for continued public support on the annual SAT results. A better indicator is probably the National Assessment of Educational Progress (NAEP), but it too has shortcomings that limit its usefulness. This federally sponsored project has gathered data on the academic achievement of American elementary and secondary students for fifteen years. But it is complex, and the results are not always well presented. Moreover, the data do not always show changes as neatly as the SAT, and not surprisingly, the NAEP receives less publicity. Finally, the data do not show state or local results but only national trends.[19]

The question is: What indicator will state officials use? Will the SAT remain the most common measure, will NAEP become more popular, or will new indicators be developed? The National Center for Education Statistics is developing a new set of education indicators to provide better evidence, a much-needed and overdue project. According to one report, this effort will include evidence on student performance; transition from one level of education to another; transition from education to the workplace; fiscal, human, and material resources; perceptions of schools; school environment; student characteristics; and state governance.[20]

Another new yardstick will soon be available because of the decision by the National Assessment of Education Progress to offer an assessment program that provides state level data. The NAEP has always provided nationally and regionally representative results on educational achievement but not data that let individual states meas-

47

ure their students' performances. Now NAEP will produce representative scores for each state and will thus allow states to compare themselves to the nation as a whole and to other states.[21]

Participation will be voluntary (and indeed states must pay for the service). The project has both benefits and drawbacks. On the one hand, it will very accurately measure students' performance and will thus provide precisely the information that state legislators and governors have wanted for many years. Its great accuracy, however, may be a problem for states that do not like the results: The NAEP design, unlike the SAT, makes it impossible to blame a poor showing on the indicator itself.

Yet another effort to develop widely accepted indicators is being launched by the Council of Chief State School Officers. Under the newly established Center for the Coordination of Educational Assessment and Evaluation, the council hopes to develop a core set of education indicators that all states would agree to adopt, thus facilitating cross-state comparisons of educational outcomes. Whether agreement on such a complex and controversial set of issues will be achieved remains to be seen, but if it is, the indicators may well provide an important benchmark for measuring educational change.

When should we see an improvement in the results? Probably the sooner the better. Unfortunately education is not a linear production function. A change of inputs does not always produce a prompt, clear change in outputs. Some observers have suggested that it may take five to ten years to produce meaningful gains. Whether the public (and elected officials) will wait that long remains to be seen. In the meantime, state leaders would do well to set clear interim goals—such as increased enrollment in math and science courses, a lower dropout rate, more highly qualified teachers, and so on—that can serve as appropriate benchmarks of progress.

Long-Term Issues

In addition to the short-term concerns mentioned above, a series of long-term issues will also shape the future of education reform. These factors include the teaching force, the balance between local autonomy and state standards, the staying power of the reform movement, and the emphasis on education for economic growth. These broader questions will ultimately determine whether the excellence movement succeeds or fails.

The Teaching Force. Many professional occupations have difficulty finding the proper balance between supply and demand. For many years, the nation had too few doctors; now it is suggested that we have too many. Similarly, there always seems to be either an undersupply or oversupply of engineers. The number is never just right. (We are, however, unaware of any suggestions that the nation has ever had a shortage of lawyers.)

The teaching profession is not immune to problems of supply and demand.[22] In the 1960s there was a serious shortage of teachers, and districts competed with each other to attract new staff. By the 1970s, however, the undersupply had become an oversupply, and many newly certified teachers were unable to find jobs. These developments affected teacher salaries. In the earlier period, school districts often bid up salaries to attract good teachers. More recently, however, the excess supply allowed school districts to underpay teachers, especially those just starting their careers. We have now reached a period where the oversupply threatens to become, once again, an undersupply. That this occurs as the nation embarks on a crash effort to improve the schools may undermine the prospects for genuine improvement.

At present the number of newly trained teachers apparently exceeds the number of job openings. Of the 132,000 college students who earned an education degree in 1981, only about 85 percent applied for teaching positions, and fewer than 70 percent found one.[23] Feistritzer's 1984 survey found that in only seven states did 80 percent or more of those receiving initial teaching certificates find full-time teaching jobs. In contrast, fourteen states estimated that fewer than 50 percent of people with new certification found full-time teaching positions.[24]

Considerable evidence, however, suggests that there is now an imbalance in teacher production, with a severe shortage in the offing. Many school districts now have difficulty finding teachers in specialized fields, especially in secondary school math and science. Many teachers are not properly certified for the subjects they teach. In 1981, according to the U.S. Department of Education, only 44 percent of all new math and science teachers and about half of all new English teachers were certified (or were eligible for certification) in their assigned subjects.[25]

Teacher shortages are becoming common. In August 1984 Los Angeles had 1,800 teacher vacancies, a shortage they overcame in part by creating an "emergency credential" that let anyone with a college degree teach in elementary schools. New York City schools were short several thousand teachers as schools were about to open.[26] The state of Georgia recruited teachers from West Germany to fill science and math teaching vacancies.[27]

The shortages experienced in certain subjects and geographic regions this year are likely to become increasingly prevalent in the next decade. Indeed several trends suggest that we may experience an acute shortage of teachers by the early 1990s.

First, the number of teachers who retire is likely to increase substantially. Many teachers who entered the labor market in the 1950s and 1960s are nearing retirement age. Both demographic and survey data suggest that about a quarter of the teachers who were employed at the start of this decade will retire before the beginning of the next.[28]

Second, the much-heralded echo of the baby boom will create growing student enrollments in the near future. The Census Bureau reports that the number of children between the ages of one and four is the highest it has been in fifteen years. Between 1984 and 2000, the nation's school-age population is expected to increase from 47 million to 53 million. This growth will not be evenly distributed. Much of it will occur in the West, the Southwest, and the Rocky Mountain states.[29]

Third, although demographic trends will increase the number of children entering schools, they will reduce the college-age population from which most potential teachers are drawn. The reason, of course, is the declining number of students who passed through school in the 1970s. Education may thus suffer a rebound effect: The declining enrollments of the 1970s becomes a shortage of newly minted teachers in the 1980s.

Fourth, teacher-training programs have had declining success in attracting academically capable students. Several recent studies have noted that students majoring in education were less academically able than their classmates, and the situation is worsening.[30] The wide publicity given to the low academic caliber of many teacher-training programs, coupled with public awareness of the low pay and poor working conditions that most teachers face, is unlikely to encourage the most talented students to pursue teaching careers.

Fifth, the exodus of women from teaching into other careers with higher pay and more status seems likely to continue. Between 1970 and 1980, the proportion of women receiving bachelor's degrees in education dropped from 36 percent to 18 percent. In 1981, the proportion fell to 17 percent.[31]

Finally, the higher standards may also limit the number of new teachers entering the labor market. As previously noted, thirty states now restrict access to teacher education programs or test new teachers before they are certified. These standards will, of course, assure that teachers are more knowledgeable and of higher quality and will, in the process, surely help raise the status of the profession. In the short run, however, the new criteria may further limit the number of individuals entering the classroom.

The real question is what happens when the limited supply of new teachers is inadequate to meet local needs. Feistritzer suggests that many school districts will be confronted with "several unsavory choices." "If there is an insufficient number of adequately prepared and fully qualified teachers available to staff the nation's schools, those schools will be either overcrowded or staffed by teachers not ready to guide developing minds in this country's finest tradition."[32] Perhaps a preview of how states will handle this pressing problem comes from Louisiana, where the state lowered the passing score on three teacher examinations—mathematics, social studies, and business education—to help fill the state's classrooms.[33]

What goes on in the classroom is at the heart of education. The public schools will never be any better than the people who staff them. One of the central themes of the reports on education was the need to raise both the standards of the teaching profession and the incentives (that is, pay, status, and working conditions) for becoming a teacher. Clearly both have been raised. Inasmuch as we have not attracted a sufficient number of good teachers for several years, however, we must raise the incentives to enter the profession even more than we raise the standards. If we have not done so and do not do so in the near future, the quality of American education is unlikely to show significant improvement.

Are the Reforms Consistent with Excellence? The recent efforts to reform education are often characterized by state attempts to define educational standards for all schools, students, and teachers. Such an approach is hardly surprising. The schools have fallen behind and elected officials have responded by specifying the achievement levels and standards to be maintained. Still, there is an important tension between autonomy at the school level and educational uniformity. Chester E. Finn summarizes the problem:

> If you want to foster the organizational characteristics associated with school effectiveness, you probably have to empower the people who staff the school to make important decisions about what happens within it. Yet if you are an elected official discontented with the current condition of education and determined to bolster school effectiveness throughout your community or state, you are probably going to prescribe uniform standards for students

and teachers and make the curriculum more specific and homogeneous, and, in the name of accountability, reduce school autonomy.[34]

The tendency to tighten school operations by imposing mandates from government agencies is not new. In recent years federal and state governments have required that schools take certain actions or achieve certain results. But this approach runs counter to much of our knowledge about education. Schools are, in the language of organizational theorists, "loosely coupled systems"; that is, their elements are attached, but the units retain their separate identity, and the connections between them may be infrequent or weak. Thus, change in one part of the system does not necessarily produce an equal movement at another point in the system. The arrangement is not by itself good or bad; it simply complicates efforts to institute large-scale changes in organizational practices. And, when changes are instituted, it is impossible to ensure that the impact will be as uniform or direct as was intended.[35]

Moreover, the research on effective schools suggests that externally imposed requirements do not contribute to good education. Excellent schools owe much to their environment: They have clear curricular goals, high expectations for students, dedicated teachers, effective discipline, and a strong emphasis on academic subjects. The recent reforms are usually imposed by policy makers some distance from the schools. In Sizer's words:

> The trend today is toward greater centralization and thus even greater scale. As state governments become more involved in the regulation of the schools, the distance between the directors and the directed has become greater, and standardization more pervasive. We hear now of schooling reduced by state edict to minimum "minutes per year." Most educational commentators are so numbed by the tradition of such authoritative top-down direction that they fail even to see the humor in such outlandish orders, much less the waste that will result from them.[36]

For Sizer, the tendency to centralize education decision making has several key defects. First, it overlooks special local conditions, particularly school-by-school differences. Second, it overemphasizes specific measurable factors. In so doing it distorts some results of education and ignores others. Third, educators are forced to establish norms that soon become universal mandates. Fourth, bureaucracies change slowly. Once regulations have been installed, change comes hard, if at all. Finally, the tendency toward hierarchical structure stifles innovation and flexibility.[37]

Finally, Finn notes that a trend toward standardization ignores the ethos or character of the school, the element that, according to Rutter and his colleagues, explained so much of a school's success. Finn writes:

> Effective schools are more like secular counterparts of religious communities than they are like army brigades, bank branches, or factory units. Members of a school community share a belief structure, a value system, a consensual rather than hierarchical governance system, and a set of common goals that blur the boundaries between their private and organizational lives.[38]

What should we do about these concerns? The answer is unclear. Both Finn and Sizer urge policy makers to give the schools maximum flexibility. Sizer writes:

> Giving teachers and students room to take full advantage of the variety among them implies that there must be substantial authority in each school. For most . . . school systems, this means the decentralization of power from central headquarters to individual schools. For state authorities, it demands the forswearing of detailed regulations for how schools should be operated. It calls for the authorities to trust teachers and principals—and believe that the more trust one places in them, the more their response will justify that trust. This trust can be tempered by judicious accreditation systems, as long as these do not reinfect the schools with the blight of standardized required practice.[39]

Asking state officials to "trust" the people who apparently caused the problems and to resist "the blight of standardized required practice" is not a very hopeful prescription. Finn's nine commandments (for example, recognize the school as the key organizational unit in public education, develop effective school-level leadership, give individual schools more budgetary authority) for resolving this tension are more specific, but are unlikely to be very actionable for state officials intent on making rapid changes.

Intellectually, the most appealing idea is carefully specified outcome measures—state achievement examinations in selected areas—that must be passed to earn a diploma. There are several straightforward models. From the French baccalaureate system we could borrow examinations, passage of which would confer degrees of different distinction. Indeed at the college level we already confer different degrees: We graduate students cum laude, magna cum laude, and summa cum laude. From the English system of A- and O-level examinations we could borrow the idea that different patterns of preparation lead to different results. Utah seems to be exploring this idea; students there can, by taking appropriate courses, receive any of three high school degrees: college entry, high interest, or technical-vocational.

Both the French and English systems rely on essay examinations—no multiple choice, machine-scored, true-or-false tests. Oral as well as written examinations are used, and they are both designed and scored by teachers. In both cases, they are built around an explicit set of curricular guidelines, including a national syllabus. In the United Kingdom, every high school graduate has read and knows Shakespeare, just as every French baccalaureate holder has read and knows Molière.[40]

Indeed, the question is not a technical one. American states can design and require examinations as a condition of earning a diploma that would simultaneously satisfy the states' need for accountability and the local schools' need for flexibility and autonomy. The Dutch system is designed precisely to accomplish this objective: state standards and personal independence. Nietzsche called it the need to reconcile "freedom and necessity."

It is clear, however, that there has historically been only weak professional interest in a solution of this kind. Such a development could be sparked by only one source—teachers. Other countries endorse national (or state) examinations, regarding them as important and worthwhile. These nations make teaching a profession with a measurable goal. In the United States, by contrast, the largest teacher organization has for many years vigorously opposed large-scale testing of students and teachers. As a result the proposal for a national teachers' examination advanced by AFT President Albert Shanker seems all the more remarkable. If it comes to pass, it contains within itself the seeds of a genuine education revolution.

The tension between the schools' need for flexibility and the states' need for control may finally be discussed constructively. People increasingly recognize that it is not a question of good principle versus bad. Both principles are valid and important. The trick is to find the proper balance between them. Policy makers have wrestled with this issue in the past and will do so in the future as they oversee the reforms already authorized and contemplate new ones.

Staying Power. Another issue that will affect the long-range future of state education reform has been noted at several points throughout this book: Will state governments continue to devote attention and financial resources to the nature and quality of the schools? Educational deterioration did not take place overnight; it was the product of gradual changes and a steady loosening of standards. A flurry of legislative activity, no matter how impressive, will not alter long-term declines. They will be reversed only by dedicated and sustained hard work.

At least two factors will limit the chances for continued attention from legislatures and state agencies. First, politicians will sooner or later move on to other problems and challenges. When they do, attention to education will suffer. Moreover, there is a natural tendency to assume that the passage of laws will fix the problem. We may recall the large number of laws passed in some states and the comprehensive nature of reform in other places. Who could fault Arkansas legislators for believing that they had solved their problems in some of the 122 laws they had enacted?

Indeed, a recent survey by the National Governors Association (NGA) makes this point. The NGA asked governors to identify the major problems they expected to face in 1985 and in 1989. Education was the most frequently cited issue in 1985, but it was rarely mentioned for 1989.[41] At least some governors apparently think they can fix the education problem and walk away from it.

Second, the actors themselves will change. Many of the reforms enacted so far have resulted from the persistence of a handful of political leaders. These officials will eventually move on to other positions or will leave politics. Will their successors remain as committed to education, or will they tackle other issues? Probably the latter. Most politicians prefer to set their own agendas rather than adopt those of their predecessors. In short, whether the education reform efforts achieve their promise will depend in large part on the policy interests of state officials who move into policy-setting positions in the second half of this decade.

The key to the states' staying power will thus be the continued interest of elected officials. School reform became possible when state legislatures and governors made a concerted effort to examine the schools and to improve them. The outpouring of new laws is unprecedented, but so are the managerial tasks that now confront state and local administrators. Withdrawal or a wavering of attention may result in backsliding and a resumption of old habits that undermine what has already been accomplished.

Education for Economic Growth. Much of the state interest in education reform was stimulated by the promise that education holds for economic growth. One participant in the Task Force on Education for Economic Growth noted, "The purpose of this task force is to link education to the economic well-being of our individual states and our nation as a whole."[42] Similarly, the National Commission on Excellence in Education observed:

> The time is long past when America's destiny was assured simply by an abundance of natural resources and inexhaustible human enthusiasm, and by our relative isolation from the malignant problems of older civilizations. The world is indeed one global village. We live among determined, well-educated and strongly motivated competitors. We compete with them for international standing and markets, not only with products but also with ideas of our laboratories and neighborhood workshops.[43]

None of the recent reports on education argue that economic progress is the sole reason for improving American education, but economic growth is clearly a major impetus behind the drive for better schools. Considerable evidence supports the claim that economic growth requires a well-educated work force. One recent analysis of human capital, for example, concluded that education is, over the long term, the single most important variable in economic growth. Carnevale writes:

> The long view of economic history teaches us that people are the master economic resource. They are the master resource because they use their acquired skills and abilities as the agents that combine tangible elements and intangible ideas to make machinery and usable goods and services. In spite of that fact, there is a great temptation . . . to ignore the long term value of human investment.[44]

Just as there is a temptation to "ignore the long term value of human investment," however, so is there a danger in suggesting that education can guarantee economic success and prosperity. Economic growth, at both the national and state level, is the product of a combination of forces that are only dimly understood. Certainly an educated and well-trained labor force is essential (and likely to be increasingly important in the future), but it is not the only factor.

The tendency to view education as a means to an end rather than as a goal in itself is not new. In the late 1950s education was seen as the way to assure national security. A decade later, education was portrayed as the way to break the cycle of poverty. In both cases education is vitally important, perhaps the single most important factor involved. It is not the only factor, however. Unfortunately, the tendency to assume that it was has contributed in some measure to a decline in public confidence in the schools as people realized that in neither case would we reach the lofty objectives we had set.

Americans have always had mixed views about the schools, about the purposes that the schools were meant to serve, and about the ways in which the schools might be structured to meet their objectives. As a result, there is no agreement about what to teach or how to teach it. Americans, being practical in nature, value the schools for their contribution to our economy or national defense. We do not value the life of the mind. As a result, intellectual discipline has never been a strong characteristic of most public schools, and recent developments, although gratifying to observers who believed that the schools had fallen behind, are not likely to make it one.

Today, however, unlike the two waves of reform in the 1950s and 1960s, new money and resources are scarce. The reforms we implement now will not be purchased in many places by wholesale funding of major new programs; the money, despite funding increases in some states, is simply not there. State governments must upgrade the schools while keeping spending in check. This dual imperative will force the states to reexamine current practice and to think of ways to use existing resources more effectively. Indeed, the states and the reformers now face this challenge as the first wave of reform passes: They must define more precisely what the schools should do without forcing them into a straightjacket of policy prescriptions. At the same time they must emphasize the importance to our national well-being of an educated citizenry as a benefit in itself, not for any short-run gain it may bring us. It is a tall order.

The Future of Education Reform: An Agenda

Whether the recent state efforts to improve education will be a passing phenomenon or a genuine transformation of elementary and secondary education remains to be seen. The result will depend largely on the actions of state policy makers in the next few years. Precisely what the states should do to maintain the impetus of reform is unclear. Defining a common set of tasks for all states is impossible. What California should do (and can do) is far different from the agenda in Mississippi. Indeed, if there were a single set of solutions equally applicable to the fifty states, the federal government would probably have pursued it.

Nevertheless, a small number of central issues must appear on state agendas. If one theme cuts across all states, it is that the long-range impact of the recent reforms will hinge on the staying power of those who launched them. Will these sponsors continue to focus on education quality, or will other issues begin to divert attention from the schools? Oversight is one of the more difficult and least rewarding forms of legislative activity, but only through such efforts can thoughtful policy adjustments be made.

States must also ensure that adequate resources are available. The passage of far-reaching reforms without provision for the funds needed to implement them invites failure and cynicism. Although substantial funding increases should not necessarily be viewed as the only factor in improving the schools, new resources will no doubt be necessary in many cases. If new money is not provided, states must be willing to reallocate funds from one area to another, always a politically difficult task.

States must also pay close attention to the new reforms' impact on minorities and disadvantaged students. States will need to study the results of statewide assessment and testing programs; making careful and thorough state data collection and analysis capabilities increasingly important. But examining the impact of the reforms is more than collecting data. In some cases it will require reopening policy debates and restructuring the initiatives launched in the last two years—a difficult task. Much of the reform legislation was passed in a rush to approve new initiatives. Any future activity will be more deliberate, built on the base of existing legislation. As a result, it is likely to prove much more difficult.

The teaching force must also be a focus of state efforts. As the supply of teachers diminishes, state and local school districts will pay increasing attention to attracting and retraining teachers. The central question will be the quality of the professionals who teach: Will they be among the best of the nation's college graduates (as they once were) or among the least capable (as they often are today)? The answer is likely to depend on incentives and on the status of the profession, both of which can be influenced by state policy makers.

Despite the central role to be played by state governments, there is an important role for both the federal government and the business community. The federal government can provide continuing pressure for reform, one that urges continual improvements in education quality. In part, this can be accomplished by using the Department of Education as a "bully pulpit" and exhorting state and local officials to act. Rhetoric alone is not sufficient, however. The federal government should encourage innovative practices and should underwrite the cost of experimental efforts that hold significant national promise. Vast new sums of money will not be required, although modest funds will be necessary. More important is the ability to discern promising innovation and to recognize that the role of the federal government is primarily supportive, not directive. This in itself is a major change in perspective.

The federal government must continue to emphasize educational programs for children with special educational needs. For the last twenty years the federal government has concentrated its education support on pupils from disadvantaged backgrounds, on handicapped pupils, and on pupils who do not speak English. Emphasis on these students has ensured that educational services would be provided to students who were often underserved by states and local school districts. These federal efforts are widely accepted and provide some assurance that appropriate educational services will be provided to all children.

The federal government also has the responsibility to gather and maintain statistics on the state of the nation's schools. Data gathering is a traditional federal role and one that is usually uncontroversial, inexpensive, and vital as a way of identifying areas of progress or difficulty. Similarly, the national government has a major role to play in sponsoring educational research. No other level of government or private sponsor has the inclination or the resources to undertake long-term basic research into the learning process.

In recent years, however, federal efforts in both data collection and research have fallen short. The National Center for Education Statistics has frequently been starved for resources. The National Institute of Education has also seen its resources dwindle. In addition, it has become the home of bizarre turf fights and has been unable to set and pursue a significant program of educational research. Neither research nor statistics is politically appealing, and there is only a small constituency for both. It is therefore easy to overlook the national interest in ensuring that both activities are adequately funded and staffed. Such a tendency should be corrected.

Yet another actor with an important role to play is the corporate community. Many businesses now make substantial efforts to support and improve the public schools. Because business is increasingly aware of its dependence on the schools for a trained work force, this interest is likely to continue and, if anything, to grow in the coming years. The schools are also increasingly aware of their need to cultivate the private sector, which provides another impetus for future collaborative relationships.

It is easy to overestimate the role that the business community might play in reforming the schools. The financial resources available for the schools from the corporate world are limited. Despite enormous increases in private sector giving, only about $50 million come from this source. This is less than 0.1 percent of the total expenditures spent on elementary-secondary education in the United States. Otherwise stated, it is about one-tenth the amount that schools raise themselves through such practices as bake sales, ticket raffles, and magazine drives. The private sector, however, like the federal government, can often command influence far beyond the dollar value of its contribution (and unlike the federal government, it does not create a regulatory burden).

In view of the variation in corporate interests, it is impossible to define with any precision the course of action that individual corporations should pursue. Similarly, the needs of nearby schools and districts on which the corporations usually focus vary considerably. The relationship between the business community and the schools must thus, of necessity, be defined by local needs, interest, and resources.

Nevertheless, it seems clear that several types of activities are especially appropriate for corporate efforts. First, corporations can provide a small amount of strategic resources to encourage the schools to undertake new and innovative activities that might not be possible without outside funding. In a sense, this would be "risk money" for special projects.

The corporate sector can also sponsor partnership arrangements that focus on particular areas of expertise or interest. Many schools and businesses, for example, have developed partnerships focused on skills that make people employable. In other cases, math, science, and technology partnerships have been launched in an effort to tap business expertise and to supplement the schools' resources.

Finally, the business community can play a leadership role in public education. When the business community speaks with one voice—as it has done in California and Minnesota—it can effect major changes in public policy. Even in more limited cases, however, evidence of business interest in the schools provides additional pressure on state and local policy makers, helping ensure that education remains high on the public policy agenda.

5
Conclusion

In this book we have discussed the states in a national context because education has always been "a national concern, a state responsibility, and a local function." The meaning of this old bromide changes with time, however, as society alters and as the responsibilities of various levels of government shift in response.

During the past twenty years, for example—because of the Great Society—many observers came to associate education reform, change, and renewal with the federal government. The national government's penchant for distributing modest amounts of funds for clearly defined purposes had a significant impact on the schools' actions. In addition, the federal government's commitment to racial equality made itself felt as no pedagogically oriented program would have done. Change, insofar as it occurred, was purchased with federal funds; it was a top-down federal strategy, accomplished by rule, regulation, statute, and appropriation. It was "trickle down" reform.

For the half century preceding the Great Society, education reform, change, and renewal was associated not with the federal government but with "lighthouse" schools and school districts run by educators who assumed prominence by virtue of their high standards and independence. Perhaps the best example of such a leader was William Cornog, the president of Central High School in Philadelphia. A classicist and humanist, Cornog was a national figure for more than three decades, playing a key role in the development of the Advanced Placement Examinations of the College Board. He completed his distinguished career as superintendent of the New Trier, Illinois, schools—to this day widely regarded as one of the nation's premier public school systems.

For more than a century before that, educational leadership was provided by individuals of great distinction—DeWitt Clinton, Horace Mann, and Henry Barnard—men who conducted successful reform campaigns that changed the face of the nation. They achieved their objectives through exhortations to excellence and by indefatigable campaigning for reform, particularly among state legislatures and state school committees. Implementation was accomplished largely through state rule, regulation, and law.

Today we have come full circle. America again looks to committed reformers to enact major reform at the state level. Indeed, there is no shortage of them. The list of governors, state legislators, chief state school officers, and state board of education members who care about genuine and lasting reform is long.

There is no guarantee, of course, that real reform will occur, or that, if it does, it will be lasting. The natural state for any organization, schools included, is a position of rest. Moreover, good education—as distinct from training—is by its nature a dynamic, tension-filled activity. Good education cannot exist in a moribund institution. If schools treat the need to restore excellence as business as usual—which they are inclined by temperament and experience to do—the prospects for reform will vanish like water poured on sand. Indeed, it is all too easy to write a scenario of missed opportunities and lost chances. We need only observe that we have the schools we want, even if they are not the schools we deserve. By any measure they have had substantial resources and flexibility; on balance they have been treated with generosity and respect. If our schools choose to value driver education as highly as trigonometry, to give power volleyball equal billing with the Greek classics in translation, they do not do so because they are inadequately funded. They do so because of their values—and those of their constituents.

If the schools do not show progress, state governments will have to explain why. Today the states have the opportunity, the responsibility, and the motives (economic growth and social progress) to change and improve education. They also have the competence and the moral authority to do so. These last two are critically important but little noted. Although it is not possible to quantify either (except in the most rudimentary way), neither attribute is the less important for it. The two are the sine qua non of political legitimacy, without which self-governance is impossible.

Consider moral authority. The greatest political triumph of the New Deal was to confer moral authority on the federal government as intervener in domestic policy. The federal government did what neither state nor local governments could do—it protected the weak and the infirm, the defenseless and the forlorn. The political economy of the New Deal was an affirmation of the responsibility of the state to the individual. By the 1960s the federal government's moral authority had been broadened to include racial and ethnic minorities, the poor, women, and the handicapped.

The modern welfare state, however, by reaching so far, over-reached, and today there is widespread reaction, not to the "safety net," nor to the appropriateness of the idea of state intervention, but to the degree and nature of the intervention. The question is not "should we intervene?"—as it once was—but "where and how should we intervene?" What interventions are most likely to be successful? At present, the preferred locus of intervention is at the state and local level.

This reaction is not confined to the United States. In the great democracies the swing of the social and political pendulum is to be expected. If the federal government is no longer viewed as the principal repository of political virtue, it is because moral authority in domestic politics is moving to the states.

In part this shift is a commentary on the federal government's success in dealing with the great moral issues of the twentieth century, economic and racial justice. The triumph of the New Deal was the development of redistributive policies that preserved the basic outlines of capitalism. The most important accomplishment of the Great Society was to make the question of race a matter for the national government. The federal government did not trust states and localities to meet their constitutional obligations to minority students and imposed its will on lower levels of government. Although much remains to be done, much has been accomplished. So much in fact, that the agenda is a closed issue. No one proposes anything but more progress.

The shift in moral authority is also explained by the increasing institutional capacity of the states. The public's confidence in state government increases because people have something about which to be confident. State governments differ greatly from the institutions of two decades ago. There is a greater willingness to address social needs and far greater competence in doing so.

In a very real sense, then, the first four years of the Reagan administration were a triumph of education policy, although hardly one that was planned. Through federal budget policy the states have been starved, not into submission, but into self-reliance. One recent analysis called this the "major sleeper issue" of the Reagan presidency, "one likely to have a substantial and lasting impact."[1] For education policy, the change is profound. As Michael Timpane, president of Columbia University's Teachers College recently said, "The attitude used to be that, if you got in trouble, the Federal Government would be available as a last resort. Now the states no longer believe that the cavalry is coming over the hill. They realize that the responsibility will continue to be theirs, and they have decided to carry it out."[2]

There is, of course, an important federal role in education. But this role suffers in part because it is so poorly conceptualized; liberals and conservatives stalk education policy from different ends of the same continuum. Their prescriptions for federal action are mirror images of each other: Liberals want more of the same, conservatives want less. Both positions are intellectually barren. Neither reflects the realities of the present.

With such uncertainty at the federal level, the institutional and policy competence of the states becomes increasingly important and increasingly recognized. For years the venality, limited intelligence, and limited vision of the states was assumed, as was the superior virtue, foresight, and competence of the federal government. No longer is it so. And as states develop the capacity to work effectively with complex and demanding issues they will develop a taste for doing so.

Once the states have gained power and responsibility, they will be reluctant to see it return to the federal government. If anything, the process of devolving responsibility for education back to the states—for whatever reason—is likely to have enormous staying power. If state governments are to be small versions of Washington—with full-time or nearly full-time legislators, large and well-qualified professional staffs, time, resources, and energy to conduct oversight and foresight hearings—they will not willingly yield authority in those areas in which they have gained it, especially in an area where the constitutional responsibility is theirs.

As matters stand, the states have made extraordinary gains in education over the past several years. In part a response to the rising tide of reports, the reform impulse was also home grown. The problems enumerated in the reports and the sense of dismay they caused led state officials to take prompt, vigorous, and often comprehensive action. The states, then, are to be commended for their enterprise and diligence. What remains to be seen is the pace, direction, and impact of the reforms already adopted. Reforms are not self-implementing, and although state reforms stand a higher chance of being successfully adopted than do many federal reforms, nothing works quite as smoothly in practice as it does on the legislative drawing board.

Trickle down reform takes time, whether the drops of change originate in Washington, Sacramento, or Nashville. As T.S. Eliot wrote: "Between the act and the reality falls the shadow." So too is it with public policy: between the law and the impact falls the shadow. That shadow is what policy analysts call implementation—the process of moving from a policy decision to a program or to policy operations. If there is a common theme to this growing literature, it is that nothing ever works as planned.

How the shadow of implementation falls is the result of many factors, some of which are within the control of elected officials: the design of the law, its flexibility, its scope and reach, the resources devoted to it, and the oversight it receives.

Less susceptible to intervention is the attitude and enthusiasm of the individuals who are called upon to act. Although a state legislature is more likely to be in tune with its local schools than the U.S. Congress, it is still an enormous distance from statehouse to schoolhouse. Similarly, state legislatures and governors (like the Congress and the president) cannot always control the events that come before them, many of which need urgent attention. Nor can the states decisively influence federal policy actions that will shape their agenda. As we have suggested, how the federal government deals with the budget deficit has profound implications for the health of the states and of education reform.

Resource scarcity will also be an issue at the state level. When the state reform impulse passes, education will find itself in vigorous competition for funding, much as it already is at the national level. Education will compete with housing, transportation, recreation, and other leisure activities. The more pressing contest, however, may pit education against education: preschool against vocational, higher against lower.

Some observers are concerned that today's preoccupation with excellence will run at cross-purposes to the nation's interest in equity. Such concern, although well motivated, is misplaced. Equity and excellence are not mutually exclusive; to the contrary, they reinforce one another. The American genius has been to reconcile liberty and equality, the precise political analogues of excellence and equity. No other society in history has done so, and it is the American vision and the American promise. The founders believed in a natural aristocracy of talent. The public schools give that belief operational expression. Only when everyone has an equal opportunity can true excellence flourish.

Equity and excellence are in conflict only if "equal outcomes" are expected. Excellence means that some students will do better than others; equity means that each will be given an equal chance. A society that fears excellence because it means unequal outcomes may be sure of one thing: That society will be neither excellent nor equal.

The commitment to high-quality education in America runs deep. One sign is the growing interest in private education. Today, in the late 1980s, we should remember the reasons that public education exists at all. Nineteenth-century reformers, beginning with Clinton, Mann, and Bernard, were convinced that the private sector could not—would not—be sufficient. Children at risk—to use today's term— were the least likely to seek and find private education. They were also most in need of good education. For this very reason the free school society became the public school society. Public funds were therefore appropriated, and the public schools so created became subject to public control. Public schooling, then, was justified by the inability of the private sector to serve a constituency in need. It was the classic justification for public intervention in a private market: market failure—an old story in health, education, and welfare.

Today, however, the tables are turned. The schools that stand accused of failure are those under public control. The accusation is that they serve the poor least well. By offering an inferior education, the schools further diminish the life chances of the poor. In this case it is important to remember the classic remedy for market failure: Find alternate providers.

The problem—and its solution—are structurally the same when the failure is in the public sector: The private sector appears. More parents are turning to the private sector. The gradual increase in private school enrollments is no accident. As more families enjoy higher incomes, have fewer children, and remain convinced of education's importance, the trend may sharply increase. Public school educators ignore the call for fundamental reform at their peril.

The bottom line is not money but the values and character of elected state officials. How they see the issues, what they choose to emphasize, their tolerance for conflict, and their willingness to continue to make tough choices are impossible to predict. Circumstance versus character is the most basic story of public policy making. It will continue to be so.

How the states move from here, and how the reforms work in practice, will have a profound impact on the future of the public schools. Many of these reforms were enacted in haste. There are design problems. Money will be in short supply. In some cases there is a lack of commitment to them. Yet despite the central role to be played by elected state officials in addressing the issues we have outlined, educators are the people on the firing line: teachers, principals, administrators, school boards, and state bureaucrats. If the reforms prove successful, there will be no shortage of people seeking to claim credit for the turnaround in the public schools. Should the reforms fall short, however, the educators and their students will be blamed, not the legislators who wrote unworkable laws and then walked away from them, nor the governors who lacked the interest or failed to urge adequate funding.

This has happened before. When it became clear that many of the Great Society's social programs would not achieve their ambitious objectives, the failure was widely attributed to program design and to the perverse incentives provided to program recipients. Bad ideas, hasty drafting, inadequate funding, and poor administration were all involved. In some cases, the problems were incorrectly diagnosed or conceptualized. Today's popular explanation is that the recipients are to blame. We are reminded of a southern governor's lament that prisons will only be improved when we get a better class of prisoner. At a minimum such explanations help to undermine public support and confidence in government.

In this vein, for better or worse, we have raised the stakes on the public schools. If commitment remains high and the steps already taken to improve them bear fruit, we may embark on an era of renewed public confidence in, and public support for, the schools. But if the reform impulse fails, or the reforms appear to fall short, confidence in the public schools will be further undermined.

Just as the opportunities for genuine and lasting reform have never been greater, so too have the dangers of failure never been more stark. The future belongs to the educated. It remains to be seen whether Americans will seize the moment for education reform.

Notes

In preparing this volume the authors benefited from the assistance and comments of Carol Herrnstadt Shulman, Forbis Jordan, Chris Pipho, Ola Clarke, and Susan Traiman. The authors alone are responsible for any errors of fact or interpretation.

Notes to Chapter 1

1. U.S. Department of Education, *The Nation Responds: Recent Efforts to Improve Education* (Washington, D.C.: Government Printing Office, 1984), p. 11.

Notes to Chapter 2

1. National Center for Education Statistics, *Digest of Education Statistics, 1983–84* (Washington, D.C., 1984), table 21, p. 27; and unpublished estimates.

2. Luther Gulick, "Reorganization of the States," *Civil Engineering* (August 1933), p. 430. Some of the evidence used in this section appeared previously in Terry W. Hartle and Richard P. Holland, "The Changing Context of Federal Education Aid," *Education and Urban Society*, vol. 15, no. 4 (August 1983), pp. 408–31.

3. Roscoe Martin, *The Cities and the Federal System* (New York: Atherton Press, 1965), pp. 45–47.

4. Terry Sanford, *Storm over the States* (New York: McGraw-Hill, 1967), p. 1.

5. The decisions were *Baker* v. *Carr* (369 U.S. 186) in 1963, *Wesberry* v. *Sanders* (376 U.S. 1) in 1964, and *Reynolds* v. *Sims* (377 U.S. 533) in 1964.

6. Jerome T. Murphy, "The Paradox of State Government Reform," *Public Interest*, no. 64 (Summer 1981), p. 126.

7. William Pound, "The State Legislatures," in *The Book of the States, 1982–83* (Lexington, Ky.: Council of State Governments, 1982), vol. 24, p. 181.

8. Larry Sabato, *Goodbye to Good-Time Charlie* (Lexington, Mass.: Lexington Books, 1978), p. 126. Thad L. Beyle, "The Governors and the Executive Branch," in *The Book of the States, 1982–83*, pp. 141–49.

9. Sabato, *Goodbye to Good-Time Charlie*, pp. 56–57.

10. Beyle, "The Governors and the Executive Branch," *The Book of the States, 1982–83*, pp. 141–49.

11. Murphy, "The Paradox of State Government Reform," p. 127.

12. The figures are drawn from the Census Bureau's 1983 Public Employee Survey. The 1983 figure includes many employees supported in part or in total by federal grants to state governments.

13. Council of State Governments, *The Book of the States, 1983–84* (Lexington, Ky.: Council of State Governments, 1984), vol. 25, pp. 341–43.

14. Murphy, "The Paradox of State Government Reform," p. 125.

15. Advisory Commission on Intergovernmental Relations, *The States and Distressed Communities* (Washington, D.C.: ACIR, 1981), p. 58.

16. Advisory Panel on the Scholastic Aptitude Test Score Decline, *On Further Examination* (New York: College Board, 1977).

17. For a discussion of the annual Gallup poll on education, see Stanley Elam, ed., *A Decade of Gallup Polls of Attitudes toward Education, 1969–1978* (Bloomington, Ind.: Phi Delta Kappa, 1978). The attitudes of parents with children in the schools are especially important because falling enrollments meant that a progressively smaller proportion of the respondents actually had children in the schools. In 1974, for example, 55 percent of the Gallup poll respondents had no children in the public schools and 39 percent did have children enrolled. Eight years later, the figures were 69 percent and 27 percent, respectively. If anything, the ratings given the schools by adults with children in them fell faster than did the ratings of the public at large.

18. Figures supplied by Chris Pipho, Education Commission of the States, Denver, Colorado. For a more comprehensive analysis of these issues, see "The Minimum Competency Testing Movement," *Phi Delta Kappan*, May 1978, pp. 585–625, a special issue edited by Chris Pipho.

19. Susan Fuhrman, "State-Level Politics and School Financing," in Nelda H. Cambron-McCabe and Allan Odden, eds., *The Changing Politics of School Finance* (Cambridge, Mass.: Ballinger Publishing Company, 1982), pp. 54–55.

20. See Richard Lehne, *The Quest for Justice* (New York: Longman, 1978).

21. Fuhrman, "State-Level Politics and School Financing," p. 54.

22. Harold R. Winslow and Susan M. Peterson, "State Initiatives for Special Needs Students," in Joel D. Sherman, Mark A. Kutner, and Kimberly J. Small, eds., *New Dimensions of the Federal-State Partnership in Education* (Washington, D.C.: Institute for Educational Leadership, 1982), p. 49.

23. Teacher union memberships provided by the American Federation of Teachers and the National Education Association. For a further discussion of these issues, see Diane Ravitch, *The Troubled Crusade: American Education, 1945–1980* (New York: Basic Books, 1983), pp. 313–16; see also Terry W. Hartle, "The Public and the Teacher Unions: Out of Step on the Basics?" *Public Opinion*, vol. 7, no. 2 (April/May 1984), pp. 55–58.

24. Quoted in Fuhrman, "State-Level Politics and School Financing," pp. 60–61.

25. James S. Coleman, et al., *Equality of Educational Opportunity* (Washington, D.C.: Government Printing Office, 1966).

26. Ravitch, *The Troubled Crusade*, p. 169.

27. Frederick Mosteller and Daniel P. Moynihan, eds., *On Equality of Educational Opportunity* (New York: Random House, 1972). Christopher Jencks et al., *Inequality: A Reassessment of the Effect of Family and Schooling in America* (New York: Basic Books, 1972).

28. James S. Coleman, Thomas Hoffer, and Sally Kilgore, *High School Achievement* (New York: Basic Books, 1982). For an illustration of the controversy spawned by this study, see "Report Analysis: Public and Private Schools," *Harvard Educational Review*, vol. 51, no. 4 (November 1981), pp. 481–545. For another discussion of the issues, see Denis P. Doyle's review essay "High School Achievement," in *Teaching Political Science*, vol. 10, no. 4 (Summer 1983), pp. 201–2.

29. Michael Rutter et al., *Fifteen Thousand Hours* (Cambridge, Mass.: Harvard University Press, 1979), p. 1.

30. Barbara Lerner, "American Education: How Are We Doing?" *Public Interest*, no. 69 (Fall 1982), pp. 59–82.

31. Sara Lawrence Lightfoot, *The Good High School* (New York: Basic Books, 1983).

32. Stewart C. Purkey and Marshall S. Smith, "Effective Schools—A Review" (Madison, Wis.: Wisconsin Center for Education Research, 1982).

33. Stanley Elam, ed., *A Decade of Gallup Polls of Attitudes toward Education, 1969–1978*. More current results are found annually in the September issue of *Phi Delta Kappan*.

34. See, for example, Chester E. Finn, Jr., "A Call for Quality Education," *Life Magazine*, March 1981, pp. 68–77.

35. National Commission on Excellence in Education, *A Nation at Risk* (Washington, D.C.: Government Printing Office, 1983), p. 5.

36. James Bryant Conant, *The American High School Today* (New York: McGraw-Hill, 1959).

37. Task Force on Education for Economic Growth, *Action for Excellence* (Denver, Colo.: Education Commission of the States, 1983), p. 14.

38. Twentieth Century Fund Task Force on Federal Elementary and Secondary Education Policy, *Making the Grade* (New York: Twentieth Century Fund, 1983).

39. National Science Board Commission on Precollege Education in Mathematics, Science, and Technology, *Educating Americans for the Twenty-first Century* (Washington, D.C.: National Science Foundation, 1983).

40. John I. Goodlad, *A Place Called School: Prospects for the Future* (New York: McGraw-Hill, 1983).

41. Theodore R. Sizer, *Horace's Compromise: The Dilemma of the American High School* (New York: Houghton Mifflin, 1984).

42. Lightfoot, *The Good High School.*

43. Ernest L. Boyer, *High School: A Report on Secondary Education in America* (New York: Harper & Row, 1983).

44. For a summary and brief analysis of the major reports, see Education Commission of the States, *A Summary of Major Reports on Education* (Denver, Colo.: Education Commission of the States, 1983); see also Marsha Levine, "School Reform: A Role for the American Business Community" (Washington, D.C.: American Enterprise Institute, 1983). A more extensive analysis appears in A. Harry Passow, *Reforming Schools in the 1980s: A Critical Review of the National Reports* (New York: Clearinghouse on Urban Education; Teachers College, Columbia University, 1984). Passow also provides an excellent summary of all the major education reform reports issued in this century.

45. Paul Peterson, "Did the Education Commissions Say Anything?" *Brookings Review* vol. 2, no. 2 (Winter 1983), p. 3. For another critical review of the education reports, see Andrew Hacker, "The Schools Flunk Out," *New York Review*, April 12, 1984, pp. 35–40.

46. Cited in Passow, *Reforming Schools in the 1980s*, p. 84.

47. Task Force on Education for Economic Growth, *Action in the States: Progress toward Education Renewal* (Denver, Colo.: Education Commission of the States, 1984), p. iv.

48. Cited in Jerome Cramer, "Some State Commandments of Excellence Ignore Reality and Undercut Local Control," *The American School Board Journal*, vol. 171, no. 9 (September 1984), p.26.

Notes to Chapter 3

1. Sizer, *Horace's Compromise*, p. 180

2. National Commission on Excellence in Education, *A Nation at Risk*, p. 22.

3. Boyer, *High School*, pp. 154–85.

4. National Center for Education Statistics, *Condition of Education, 1982* (Washington, D.C.: Government Printing Office, n.d.), table 3.7, chart 3.7, pp. 102–3.

5. Sizer, *Horace's Compromise*, p. 180.

6. Robert Palaich and Ellen Flannelly, "Improving Classroom Teaching through Incentives" (Denver, Colo.: Education Commission of the States, April 1984). See also Susan J. Rosenholtz, "Political Myths about Reforming Teaching" (Denver, Colo.: Education Commission of the States, 1984).

7. Harry P. Hatry and John M. Geiner, *Issues in Teacher Incentive Plans* (Washington, D.C.: Urban Institute, 1984).

8. U.S. Department of Education, *Nation Responds*, p. 127.

9. State of South Carolina, *The New Approach to Educational and Economic Excellence in South Carolina* (Columbia: Office of the Governor, n.d.).

10. U.S. Department of Education, *Nation Responds*, p. 45.

11. Task Force on Education for Economic Growth, *Action in the States* (Denver, Colo.: Education Commission of the States, 1984), pp. 24–25. See also Jim O'Hara, "Tennessee Legislature Passes Master-Teacher Bill," *Education Week*, February 29, 1984.

12. U.S. Department of Education, *Nation Responds*, p. 32.

13. J. T. Sandefur, "State Assessment Trends," *American Association of Colleges for Teacher Education Briefs*, March 1984, p. 17.

14. Ibid.

15. U.S. Department of Education, *Nation Responds*, p. 32.

16. "New Jersey Commission Details Training for Alternative Certification," *Education Times*, May 14, 1984, p. 5.

17. Allan Odden and Van Dougherty, *Education Finance in the States: 1984* (Denver, Colo.: Education Commission of the States, 1984), p. 5.

18. U.S. Department of Education, "Recent Initiatives Reported by States and the District of Columbia" (Washington, D.C.: USDE, 1984).

19. Task Force on Education for Economic Growth, *Action in the States*, pp. 21–22.

20. Ralph D. Turlington, *Focus on Public Education*, Annual Report of the Commissioner of Education (Tallahassee: State of Florida, 1984), p. 9.

21. U.S. Department of Education, "Recent Initiatives."

22. U.S. Department of Education, *Nation Responds*.

23. Chris Pipho, "Tracking the Reforms, Part 3: Principals' Academies—Training the Leaders," (Denver, Colo.: Education Commission of the States, 1985).

24. National Commission on Excellence, *A Nation at Risk*, p. 18.

25. Task Force on Education for Economic Growth, *Action for Excellence*, p. 38.

26. National Science Board, *Educating Americans for the Twenty-first Century*, p. 1.

27. Ibid., p. vi.

28. Twentieth Century Fund, *Making the Grade*, p. 14.

29. Quoted in Chester E. Finn, Jr., "The Drive for Educational Excellence," *Change Magazine*, April 1983, p. 17.

30. U.S. Department of Education, "Recent Initiatives."

31. U.S. Department of Education, *Nation Responds*, p. 46.

32. Ibid., p. 54.

33. Ibid., p. 66.

34. Ibid., p. 130.

35. Ibid., p. 126.

36. Odden and Dougherty, *Education Finance in the States*, p. 17; U.S. Department of Education, *Nation Responds*, p. 31.

37. Chris Pipho and Connie Hadley, "State Activity—Minimum Competency Test-

ing," *ECS Clearinghouse Notes* (Denver, Colo.: Education Commission of the States, 1984), xerox.

38. U.S. Department of Education, "Recent Initiatives."

39. U.S. Department of Education, *Nation Responds*, p. 28.

40. Ibid., p. 115.

41. Ibid., p. 97.

42. Ibid., p. 92.

43. U.S. Department of Education, "Recent Initiatives."

44. U.S. Department of Education, *Nation Responds*, p. 111.

45. Ibid., p. 135.

46. "Special Session Report," *The Texas Observer*, July 13, 1984, pp. 3–9.

47. Odden and Dougherty, *Education Finance in the States*, p. 17.

48. U.S. Department of Education, *Nation Responds*, p. 95.

49. State of South Carolina, *The New Approach to Educational and Economic Excellence in South Carolina*.

50. U.S. Department of Education, "Recent Initiatives."

51. U.S. Department of Education, *Nation Responds*, p. 83.

52. Ibid., p. 100.

53. National Commission on Excellence, *A Nation at Risk*, p. 33.

54. Twentieth Century Fund, *Making the Grade*, p. 22.

55. Task Force on Education for Economic Growth, *Action for Excellence*, p. 36.

56. Boyer, *High School*, p. 296.

57. National Science Board, *Educating Americans for the Twenty-first Century*, appendix C, pp. 104–14.

58. Allan Odden, "Financing Educational Excellence," *Phi Delta Kappan*, January 1984, p. 315.

59. Task Force on Education for Economic Growth, *Action in the States*, pp. 15–19.

60. Ibid., pp. 17–18.

61. U.S. Department of Education, *Nation Responds*. The tax increase in Texas was the first major hike in that state in thirteen years. See Georganne O'Connor, "Texas Governor Signs Sweeping Education Reforms," *Education Times*, July 16, 1984, p. 1.

62. Odden and Dougherty, *Education Finance in the States*, p. 8. Florida originally used a unitary tax—a tax on the worldwide profits firms earn in other countries—to raise funds for education reform. In December 1984 that tax was replaced with an increase in the state's corporate tax rate. See "Florida May End Worldwide Corporate Tax," *New York Times*, December 2, 1984; "Florida's Legislature Repeals Unitary Tax, Raises Firms' Tax Rate," *Wall Street Journal*, December 10, 1984.

63. U.S. Department of Education, *Nation Responds*, p. 65.

64. Odden and Dougherty, *Education Finance in the States*, pp. 18–19.

65. Linda Chion-Kenney, "California High Court Bans Schools' Use of Fees for Extracurriculars," *Education Week*, May 2, 1984, p. 1.

66. "Kentucky Forms State Foundation for Public Schools," *Education Week*, May 2, 1984, p. 3.

67. Task Force on Education for Economic Growth, *Action in the States*, p. 14.

68. See Henry Olson, "Campaign Heats Up in California," *Initiative and Referendum Report*, October 19, 1984, pp. 2–3; see also *Initiative News Report*, August 10, 1984, pp. 8–9.

69. U.S. Department of Education, *Nation Responds*, p. 16.

70. Ibid.

71. Task Force on Education for Economic Growth, *Action in the States*, p. 12.

72. Ibid.

73. National Commission on Excellence, *A Nation at Risk*, p. 21.

74. Ibid., pp. 29–30.

75. Boyer, *High School*, p. 142.

76. Task Force on Education for Economic Growth, *Action for Excellence*, p. 38.

77. See, for example, Chester E. Finn, Jr., Testimony before the U.S. Senate Committee on Labor and Human Resources, *Quality of Education, 1983*, Senate Hearings, 98–562, Part 2, November 2, 1983, pp. 204–22, November 2, 1983. See also Merry I. White, "Japanese Education: How Do They Do It?" *Public Interest*, no. 76 (Summer 1974), pp. 87–101.

78. National Science Board, *Educating Americans for the Twenty-first Century*, p. 39.

79. Task Force on Education for Economic Growth, *Action for Excellence*, p. 38.

80. U.S. Department of Education, "Recent Initiatives."

81. Connie Hadley, "School Calendar," *ECS Clearinghouse Notes* (Denver, Colo.: Education Commission of the States, July 1984), xerox.

82. U.S. Department of Education, *Nation Responds*, p. 76.

83. Ibid., p. 31.

84. Ibid., p. 93.

85. Ibid., various references.

86. Ibid., p. 62.

87. Ibid.

88. Hope Aldrich, "North Carolina Districts Extend School Year to 200 Days," *Education Week*, July 27, 1983, p. 8.

89. Blake Rodman, "North Carolina School District Drops Longer School Year, Day Experiment," *Education Week*, January 23, 1985, p. 5.

90. U.S. Department of Education, *Nation Responds*, p. 126.

91. Connie Hadley, "Academic Bankruptcy," *ECS Clearinghouse Notes* (Denver, Colo.: Education Commission of the States, 1984), xerox.

92. Ibid.

93. Georganne O'Connor, "Texas Governor Signs Sweeping Education Reforms Passed in Special Session of State Legislature," *Education Times*, July 16, 1984, p. 1; Georganne O'Connor, "Texas Governor Appoints Interim Board as Districts Spend New State Funds," *Education Times*, September 10, 1984, p. 1.

94. U.S. Department of Education, "Recent Initiatives."

95. U.S. Department of Education, *Nation Responds*, p. 80.

96. Ibid., p. 136

97. Alina Tugend, "Half of Florida Districts, Citing Bias, Shun 'Merit School' Program," *Education Week*, October, 3, 1984, p. 5.

98. The president's remarks are contained in "Remarks on Receiving the Final Report of the National Commission on Excellence in Education," *Public Papers of the Presidents*, Ronald Reagan, vol. 1, 1983 (Washington, D.C.: Government Printing Office, 1984), pp. 584–86.

Notes to Chapter 4

1. George Gallup, "The Gallup Poll of Teachers' Attitudes toward the Public Schools," *Phi Delta Kappan*, September 1984, pp. 23–27.

2. Jerome Cramer, "Some State Commandments of Excellence Ignore Reality and Undercut Local Control," p. 26.

3. Ibid., see also Arkansas School Boards Association, "Education Gets Historic Attention," *The Reporter*, Little Rock, Arkansas, December 1983.

4. See Jerome Cramer, "Some State Commandments of Excellence Ignore Reality and Undercut Local Control."

5. Quoted in Edward B. Fiske, "Concern over Schools Spurs Extensive Efforts at Reform," *New York Times*, September 9, 1984.

6. Denis P. Doyle and Chester E. Finn, Jr., "American Schools and the Future of Local Control," *Public Interest*, no. 77 (Fall 1984), pp. 85–86.

7. Chester E. Finn, Jr., "The Excellence Backlash: Sources of Resistance to Educational Reform," *American Spectator*, September 1984, pp. 10–16.

8. See, for example, Robert Pear, "Conflict Looming over a U.S. View on Aid for States," *New York Times*, November 25, 1984.

9. David Shribman, "Is the U.S. Tax Revolt Ending?" *Wall Street Journal*, November 27, 1984.

10. In January 1985, the Connecticut Supreme Court upheld the constitutionality of the state's finance system but ordered a lower court to determine whether recent changes in the school aid program, including funding delays, deny students an equal educational opportunity.

11. See, for example, Archie E. Lapointe, "The Good News about American Education," *Phi Delta Kappan*, June 1984, pp. 663–67. See also Launor F. Carter, "The Sustaining Effects Study of Compensatory and Elementary Education," *Educational Reseacher*, August/September 1984, pp. 4–13.

12. Sheppard Ranbom, "Higher Standards Linked to Dropout Increase," *Education Week*, April 18, 1984, p. 1.

13. Thomas Toch, "The Dark Side of the Excellence Movement," *Phi Delta Kappan*, November 1984, pp. 173–76.

14. National Coalition of Advocates for Students, *Barriers to Excellence: Our Children at Risk* (Boston: National Coalition of Advocates for Students, 1985).

15. Odden and Dougherty, *Education Finance in the States*, pp. 20–21.

16. See, for example, Finn, "The Excellence Backlash," pp. 14–15.

17. "Appeals Court Okays Florida Competency Test," *Education Daily*, May 3, 1984, p. 1.

18. Barbara Lerner, "A Consumer's Guide to a National Census of Educational Quality" (Princeton, N.J.: Lerner Associates, 1984). Lerner concedes that the SAT has shortcomings but argues that norm-referenced tests such as the SAT will reveal changes in student performance earlier and more clearly than criterion-referenced tests such as the National Assessment of Educational Progress.

19. The major differences between the SAT and the NAEP are important. SAT is taken by a self-selected population; not all high school students take it. NAEP is a nationally representative sample that oversamples certain population subgroups. Moreover, only high school students take the SAT, whereas the NAEP is given to students who are nine, thirteen, and seventeen years old.

20. Tom Mirga, "Education Department Developing New Measures of Schools," *Education Week*, October 17, 1984, p. 1.

21. "National Assessment to Provide State, Local Comparisons," *Education Week*, October 24, 1984, p. 2.

22. There are a number of good studies and compilations of evidence about the teaching force. For an overview, see Denis P. Doyle, "Window of Opportunity," *Wilson Quarterly*, vol. 8, no. 1 (Winter 1984). The most comprehensive are both by C. Emily Feistritzer: *The American Teacher* (1983) and *The Making of a Teacher* (1984). Both were published by the National Center for Education Information in Washington, D.C. Other summaries of issues related to teachers and teaching include Linda Darling-Hammond, *Beyond the Commission Reports* (Santa Monica, Calif.: Rand Corporation,

1984); Susan J. Rosenholtz and Susan J. Kyle, "Teacher Isolation: Barrier to Professionalism," *American Educator*, vol. 8, no. 4 (Winter 1984), pp. 10–15; Thomas Toch, "How to Attract Better Teachers," *Journal of Contemporary Studies*, vol. 7, no. 3 (Summer 1984), pp. 59–67; William H. Wilken, "Teacher Compensation: The Need for a New Direction," prepared by the Committee for Economic Development" (Washington, D.C.: Committee for Economic Development, 1984).

23. Wilken, "Teacher Compensation: Need for a New Direction," p. 15.

24. Feistritzer, *The Making of a Teacher*, p. 47.

25. National Center for Education Statistics, *The Condition of Education 1983* (Washington, D.C.: Government Printing Office, 1983), table 4.14, p. 206.

26. Thomas Toch, "Teacher Shortage Imperils Reform, New Study Says," *Education Week*, August 22, 1984, p. 1.

27. "Foreign Imports Ease Georgia Teacher Shortage," *Education Week*, August 22, 1984, p. 15.

28. Wilken, "Teacher Compensation: Need for a New Direction," p. 18.

29. Ibid.

30. Feistritzer, *The American Teacher*, p. 56.

31. Darling-Hammond, "Beyond the Commission Reports," p. 8.

32. Feistritzer, *The American Teacher*, p. 59.

33. At the same time, the state raised the passing score on the English certificate examination.

34. Chester E. Finn, Jr., "Toward Strategic Independence: Nine Commandments for Enhancing School Effectiveness," *Phi Delta Kappan*, April 1984, p. 518. Our discussion draws on Finn's thoughtful and detailed treatment of this issue.

35. Ibid.

36. Sizer, *Horace's Compromise*, p. 206.

37. Ibid., pp. 207–9.

38. Finn, *Toward Strategic Independence*, p. 519.

39. Sizer, *Horace's Compromise*, p. 214.

40. The notion of a national curriculum in the United States is, of course, anathema to many educators and public officials. In reality, however, there is a very common curriculum, especially at the secondary school level. James Conant once noted that while doing the field work for *The American High School* he attended chemistry classes in the schools he visited and "never missed a class" as he traveled across country. Today, textbooks usually provide a similar sequence of topics and issues for students in most schools or at least cover the same broad themes. Finally, the Advanced Placement (AP) courses taken by academically able high school students who hope to pass AP exams are very similar, regardless of where they are taught.

41. Cited in "Governors Rank Education as Chief Issue Their States Must Face This Year," *Chronicle of Higher Education*, August 8, 1984, p. 17.

42. Task Force on Education for Economic Growth, *Action for Excellence*, p. 5.

43. National Committee on Excellence in Education, *Nation at Risk*, p. 6.

44. Anthony Patrick Carnevale, *Human Capital: A High Yield Corporate Investment* (Washington, D.C.: American Society for Training and Development, 1983), p. 51.

Notes to Chapter 5

1. Richard P. Nathan and Fred C. Doolittle, "The Untold Story of Reagan's 'New Federalism,'" *Public Interest*, no. 77 (Fall 1984), pp. 96–105.

2. Quoted in Edward B. Fiske, " States Gain Wider Influence on School Policy," *New York Times*, December 2, 1984.

SELECTED AEI PUBLICATIONS

The Private Sector in the Public School: Can It Improve Education? Marsha Levine, ed. (1985, 77 pp., $4.95)

Aliteracy: People Who Can Read But Won't, Nick Thimmesch, ed. (1984, 59 pp., $3.95)

Religion and the Constitution, John Charles Daly, mod. (1984, 34 pp., $3.75)

Meeting Human Needs: Toward a New Public Philosophy, Jack A. Meyer, ed. (1982, 469 pp., cloth $34.95, paper $13.95)

Debating National Education Policy: The Question of Standards (1981, 152 pp., $6.25)

The Urban Crisis: Can Grass-Roots Groups Succeed Where Government Has Failed? John Charles Daly, mod. (1981, 25 pp., $3.75)

Church, State, and Public Policy: The New Shape of the Church-State Debate, Jay Mechling, ed. (1978, 119 pp., cloth $12.95, paper $5.25)

To Empower People: The Role of Mediating Structures in Public Policy, Peter L. Berger and Richard John Neuhaus (1977, 45 pp., $3.25)

• *Mail orders for publications to:* AMERICAN ENTERPRISE INSTITUTE, 1150 Seventeenth Street, N.W., Washington, D.C. 20036 • *For postage and handling, add 10 percent of total; minimum charge $2, maximum $10 (no charge on prepaid orders)* • *For information on orders, or to expedite service, call toll free 800-424-2873 (in Washington, D.C., 202-862-5869)* • *Prices subject to change without notice.* • *Payable in U.S. currency through U.S. banks only*

AEI ASSOCIATES PROGRAM

The American Enterprise Institute invites your participation in the competition of ideas through its AEI Associates Program. This program has two objectives: (1) to extend public familiarity with contemporary issues; and (2) to increase research on these issues and disseminate the results to policy makers, the academic community, journalists, and others who help shape public policies. The areas studied by AEI include Economic Policy, Education Policy, Energy Policy, Fiscal Policy, Government Regulation, Health Policy, International Programs, Legal Policy, National Defense Studies, Political and Social Processes, and Religion, Philosophy, and Public Policy. For the $49 annual fee, Associates receive
- a subscription to *Memorandum*, the newsletter on all AEI activities
- the AEI publications catalog and all supplements
- a 30 percent discount on all AEI books
- a 40 percent discount for certain seminars on key issues
- subscriptions to any two of the following publications: *Public Opinion*, a bimonthly magazine exploring trends and implications of public opinion on social and public policy questions; *Regulation*, a bimonthly journal examining all aspects of government regulation of society; and *AEI Economist*, a monthly newsletter analyzing current economic issues and evaluating future trends (or for all three publications, send an additional $12).

Call 202/862-6446 or write: AMERICAN ENTERPRISE INSTITUTE
1150 Seventeenth Street, N.W., Suite 301, Washington, D.C. 20036